Classics

HULL

RUGBY LEAGUE FOOTBALL CLUB

Classics

HULL

RUGBY LEAGUE FOOTBALL CLUB

RAYMOND FLETCHER

TEMPUS

To my wife, Muriel. A real old faithful pal
of mine in any kind of weather.

Frontispiece: Lee Crooks on the attack with David Topliss in
close support during the 1982 Rugby League Challenge Cup
final replay.

First published 2003

Tempus Publishing Limited
The Mill, Brimscombe Port,
Stroud, Gloucestershire, GL5 2QG

British Library Cataloguing in Publication Data.
A catalogue record for this book is available from the British Library.

ISBN 0 7524 2957 4

Typesetting and origination by Tempus Publishing Limited
Printed in Great Britain by Midway Colour Print, Wiltshire

Foreword

I suppose I must have played in several great matches for Hull, but at the time I did not appreciate it. You are so involved in the game that the matches fly by and it is only later that you begin to realise that maybe you had taken part in something special. That's when fans come up to you and say 'I remember when you' did this or that in a game, that will live long in their memory.

Now that I have long been retired I can look back on those games and think, yes, they were great. Very often it was the occasion as much as the actual match that made them special. Although I never won at Wembley in a Cup final they were all special occasions. Then there was the Challenge Cup final replay win at Elland Road that I said at the time was the happiest moment in my Rugby League life. It had everything: it was a great occasion, a great match and a great feeling to be captain of the first Hull team to win the Cup for so many years.

Another thing that added to those big occasions was the support we received from the Hull fans. To hear them singing *Old Faithful*, especially in Cup finals, always gave us a big lift. I reckon I've played in about half-a-dozen of the matches listed in this book and it gives me great pride to see them linked with other great Hull matches of the last 100 years or so.

David Topliss
Hull and Great Britain

April 2003

Classic Matches

1895 *v.* Batley   (League)

1895 *v.* Liversedge   (League)

1899 *v.* Hull K.R.   (League)

1909 *v.* Australia   (Tour)

1914 *v.* Wakefield T.   (Rugby League Cup final)

1920 *v.* Huddersfield   (Championship final)

1920 *v.* Hull K.R.   (Yorkshire Cup final)

1921 *v.* Hull K.R.   (Championship final)

1922 *v.* Rochdale H.   (Rugby League Cup final)

1923 *v.* Huddersfield   (Yorkshire Cup final)

1936 *v.* Leeds   (Rugby League Cup round 3)

1936 *v.* Widnes   (Championship final)

1936 *v.* Wigan   (League)

1953 *v.* Hull K.R.   (League)

1954 *v.* Workington T.   (Rugby League Cup round 2)

1954 *v.* Huddersfield   (Yorkshire Cup round 2 replay)

1954 *v.* Halifax   (Yorkshire Cup final)

1955 *v.* Halifax   (Yorkshire Cup final)

1956 *v.* Warrington   (Championship semi-final)

1956 *v.* Halifax   (Championship final)

1957 *v.* York   (League)

1957 *v.* Albi   (European Championship)

1957 *v.* Barrow   (Championship semi-final)

1957 *v.* Oldham   (Championship final)

1958 *v.* Oldham   (Championship semi-final)

1958 *v.* Workington T.   (Championship final)

1959 *v.* Featherstone R.   (Rugby League Cup semi-final)

1959 *v.* Wigan   (Rugby League Cup final)

1960 *v.* Wakefield T.   (Rugby League Cup final)

1969 *v.* Featherstone R.   (Yorkshire Cup final)

1974 *v.* Leeds   (Yorkshire Cup round 2)

1975 *v.* Leeds   (Players' No. 6 round 2 replay)

1976 *v.* Widnes   (Players' No 6 final)

1979 *v.* New Hunslet   (League)

1979 *v.* Hull K.R.   (Floodlit Trophy final)

1980 *v.* Hull K.R.   (Rugby League Cup final)

1982 *v.* Hull K.R.   (John Player final)

1982 *v.* Widnes   (Rugby League Cup final)

1982 *v.* Widnes   (Rugby League Cup final replay)

1982 *v.* Bradford N.   (Yorkshire Cup final)

1982 *v.* Australia 13   (Tour)

1983 *v.* Featherstone Rovers   (Rugby League Cup final)

1983 *v.* Castleford   (Yorkshire Cup final)

1984 *v.* Hull K.R.   (Yorkshire Cup final)

1985 *v.* Castleford   (Rugby League Cup semi-final replay)

1985 *v.* Wigan   (Rugby League Cup final)

1985 *v.* New Zealand 33   (Tour)

1991 *v.* Widnes   (Premiership final)

1999 *v.* Halifax Blue Sox   (Super League)

2002 *v.* New Zealand   (Tour)

Acknowledgements

First to be acknowledged must be the journalists whose reports I have spent many hours reading in researching this book. Even in this age of video, their words brought to life matches going back over a century. Several national newspapers were consulted, but it was the *Hull Daily Mail* and *Yorkshire Post* that were the greatest source of information. I am also indebted to them for many of the photographs reproduced here.

Others that have provided photographs are the *Rugby Leaguer and League Express*, with particular thanks to photographers Andrew Varley and Andy Howard. Robert Gate and Les Hoole have also been willing to provide copies from their private collections.

Special thanks also to David Topliss for the foreword. 'Toppo' played in seven of the *Classic* matches and was Hull's captain in probably their greatest era.

Finally, I would like to mention my elder sister Joyce, who took me as a schoolboy to my first Yorkshire Cup final at Leeds, and to a few other matches that are remembered in this book. Joyce died just before I completed the final chapter.

A happy bunch of Hull players show off the Yorkshire Cup after their defeat of Hull Kingston Rovers in 1984.

Introduction

In choosing the fifty matches for this book I needed to extend the meaning of the word 'classic' so that I could include those that were memorable or eventful for various reasons. In many instances the matches were indeed classics, matches of wonderful free-flowing play that makes Rugby League the greatest game of all. But some were chosen for less glorious reasons – even for their notoriety. Whenever fans get talking about memorable matches you can be sure they will recall many a pitched battle. I have even included one match that produced a slow handclap in response to the opposition's boring tactics. Read about Hull's 1954 Cup tie against Workington Town for the historic significance of that match.

Other matches are included for more pleasurable historic occasions, such as the first and last matches at The Boulevard. All fifteen of Hull's Cup and Championship-winning finals are also recalled and what a pleasure it was reliving those. Not so easy to recall were the heart-breaking trips to Wembley and a few other Cup final defeats. They were all unforgettable, albeit for the wrong reasons.

I was at thirty-four of the chosen matches and most of those were during my twenty years as the *Yorkshire Post* Rugby League correspondent, but I have also recalled a few matches that I saw as a youngster and have never forgotten. Fears that I may have then been just an easily impressed schoolboy were allayed when I looked back at the match reports and saw them described as real classics.

Raymond Fletcher

Steve Norton on the attack with Tony Dean standing by during Hull's RL Challenge Cup replay Victory over Widnes 1982.

HULL v. BATLEY

7 September 1895   League match
Mount Pleasant, Batley

'On Saturday, the Hull Football Club commenced their career under the control of the Northern Union by encountering Batley at Mount Pleasant.' That was the matter-of-fact way the *Hull Daily Mail* began its report of Hull's momentous first match after twenty-two clubs broke away from the English Rugby Union and set out on the path that was to lead to the new code of Rugby League. The club had been formed in 1865 and were respected members of the English Rugby Union until they voted in favour of a breakaway at the historical meeting at the George Hotel, Huddersfield, on 29 August 1895.

Events moved quickly after that, and only nine days later the first Northern Union matches took place with Hull's match at Batley being one of the top games of the day. The match itself was slow getting underway. Though Charles Lempriere led Hull on to the field at 3.30 p.m., Batley did not follow them for almost another twenty minutes and the kick-off finally came at 3.50 p.m. The delay proved welcome as the weather was extremely hot in the afternoon until a breeze cooled things down a little in the early evening. There was said to be 'a good attendance, not withstanding the severe heat, the weather being much more suitable for gentle summer pastimes than football.'

Although one of the major causes of the Northern clubs' breakaway was over broken-time payment for players who had to take time off work to play, it is interesting to note that William Herbert Wiles, a Hull forward, sent word that business prevented him from travelling to the game. The broken-time payment was six shillings, and Hull's total payout for the season was £195.

The *Hull Daily Mail* reported the opening moments of Hull's historic first Northern Union match thus: 'Hull won the toss, and at ten minutes to four Shackleton kicked off, and no return was made. Batley got the ball out of a scrimmage, but Charlie Townend was round like lightning, and brought off a grand tackle. Batley were penalised, and Jack Townend kicked to the home full-back, who replied into touch near the centre. Jack Townend immediately afterwards brought off a penalty kick into touch in the home quarters.'

The game was still Rugby Union, of course, and kicking continued to dominate the exchanges until a drop goal – then worth four points – was to send Hull to defeat in this historic match. But before then Jack Holmes gained the honour of becoming the first Hull player to score a try in the Northern Union. George Jacketts was prominent with a dribble and then Booth broke away with a powerful charge followed by almost the entire team in support. When the ball was moved out wide Holmes was there to score in the corner. Duncan Wright just failed to land Hull's first Northern Union goal.

Batley tried to hit back immediately, only for Charles Townend to thwart them with some good defensive work. His brother, Jack, also produced a great tackle when Batley began a threatening forward charge as Hull came under increasing pressure. Charles Townend added some fine attacking play to his defensive efforts and stood out as one of Hull's best players. Jacketts and William Jacques were also well to the fore and the 'Third-porters', as they were sometimes known, seemed to have the game well in command.

Hull 3
Try: Holmes

Batley 7
Try: Spurr
Drop goal: Shaw

The League table at the end of the first Northern Union season.

		P	W	D	L	F	A	Pts
1	Manningham	42	33	0	9	367	158	66
2	Halifax	42	30	5	7	312	139	65
3	Runcorn	42	24	8	10	314	143	56
4	Oldham	42	27	2	13	374	194	56
5	Brighouse R.	42	22	9	11	247	129	53
6	Tyldesley	42	21	8	13	260	164	50
7	Hunslet	42	24	2	16	279	207	50
8	Hull	42	23	3	16	259	158	49
9	Leigh	42	21	4	17	214	269	46
10	Wigan	42	19	7	16	245	147	45
11	Bradford	42	18	9	15	254	175	45
12	Leeds	42	20	3	19	258	247	43
13	Warrington	42	17	5	20	198	240	39
14	St. Helens*	42	15	8	19	195	230	36
15	Liversedge	42	15	4	23	261	355	34
16	Widnes	42	14	4	24	177	323	32
17	Stockport	42	12	8	22	171	315	32
18	Batley	42	12	7	23	137	298	31
19	Wakefield T.	42	13	4	25	156	318	30
20	Huddersfield	42	10	4	28	194	274	24
21	Broughton R.	42	8	8	26	165	244	24
22	Rochdale H.	42	4	8	30	78	388	16

*Deducted 2 points for playing ineligible player.

They had a good chance to go further ahead when Batley were penalised and Lempriere put in a well-placed long kick across field. Walt Mansell was first to the ball, but knocked-on with Batley's defence scattered all over. The miss was to prove a costly one as Hull never came so close to scoring again.

It was not until late in the first half that Batley put Hull under any real pressure, but the visitors held out to take a deserved 3-0 interval lead. Dribbling was a feature of the early Northern Union matches and both teams put it to good use in relieving pressure from deep inside their own half. Lempriere also got Hull out of trouble with a long touchline run as Batley started to get on top. Not long after this relieving breakaway, Batley drew level when Hull conceded their first Northern Union try. Following an exchange of deep kicks, Batley forced their way up field and Spurr dashed in for the touchdown, Joe Naylor failing with the kick.

It was now 3-3 and the closing stages created great excitement for the crowd as reported by the *Hull Daily Mail*: 'Hull dropped out and after the usual exchange, Johnson was tackled with the ball inside his own 25. Batley were now playing with more dash, and took the play right to the Hull line. The position was critical, but Hull looked like escaping, when the ball went out to Shaw, who dropped a terribly lucky goal. Jacketts, after the serious reverse, re-started and play settled down in Hull's 25. Hull was awarded a free kick, and Mansell kicked into touch near the 25 flag. When the ball came loose, Batley again seemed the more aggressive, but Johnson cleared. It now only wanted three or four minutes to time, and Hull's chance of wiping off the adverse balance was apparently hopeless. The end came, Hull being beaten by a dropped goal.'

Hull: Johnson; Lempriere, Jacques, J. Townend, Wright; C. Townend, G. Barker; Mansell, Booth, Feetham, Holmes, Harmer, Carr, F. Spenceley, Jacketts.

Batley: Lane; Shaw, J. Goodall, Joe Naylor, Oakland; Jim Naylor, Elliker; Shackleton, Munns, Fisher, Littlewood, Wilby, Stubley, Spurr, Welsh.

HULL v. LIVERSEDGE

21 September 1895   League match
The Boulevard, Hull

Welcome to The Boulevard. Hull's first match at their famous old ground was hailed as the beginning of a great new era for the club, and victory over one of the top sides in the Northern Union gave it a wonderful send-off. Hull had moved to the Athletic Ground, as it was called then, and forced out rivals Hull Kingston Rovers after agreeing to pay triple the £50 a year rental. It was not until 1899 that Hull bought the ground for £6,500 and officially renamed it The Boulevard. The original move provoked much controversy, as many felt Hull were deserting their East Hull fans by moving across the city. But a record crowd (for that time) for a rugby match in the city of about 8,000 packed into the ground on a sunny September afternoon. Admission was threepence or ninepence to the main stand, and the local press described the attendance as 'tremendous'.

'The attendance was as large as it was fashionable and influential,' said one report. 'Altogether the ground presented a very grand and imposing appearance, whilst there was plenty of cheering and excitement when to the lively strains of the East Hull Band the chosen gladiators came tripping out on the green at 3.35 p.m.'

It was only the third weekend of matches under the newly-formed Northern Union following their momentous split from the English Rugby Union. Hull had played two away matches, losing their opening fixture 7-3 at Batley and gaining a surprise 9-3 win at Warrington. It was still fifteen-aside under Rugby Union rules and Hull's Plugge was praised for being 'a terror in the line-outs'. Low scoring was very much the pattern of most games and this one was to be no exception. No points were scored in the first forty minutes and the only score did not come until early in the second half when George Jacketts had the distinction of scoring the first ever try at The Boulevard. The *Hull Daily Mail* reported the start of the second half and build-up to the try thus:

'After a little more music and refreshment for the players, Sharpe, for the latter, resumed with the wind strengthening behind the backs of the home players, for whom Thompson made the running by kicking well up to Hallas, who preferred to let the ball roll dead. After the drop-out, Johnson showed a good turn of speed, which carried him to the visitors' 25, where he gave up to Mahoney, who was forthwith pushed into touch. In the lineout the home forwards were seen to more advantage and C. Towend passing right across to Lempriere, the latter struggled hard to get through a crowd of opponents before giving up possession to Thompson. Herbert was immediately brought down, but Wiles had secured the oval with which he rushed towards the line. Hallas tackled gamely, and Wiles throwing the oval to Jacketts, the veteran registered Hull's first try amidst a chorus of cheering. G. Barker failed to improve the value.'

Charles Lempriere had the honour of leading Hull out for the historic match that had a ceremonial kick-off carried out by Arthur Wilson, the Master of Hounds from Tranby Croft (There would not be too many of those on Hessle Road). Hull won the toss and after Mr Wilson had performed his duty, the match was restarted with a scrum. Kicking and scrums dominated the first forty minutes with only the

---

Hull 3   **Liversedge 0**
  Try: Jacketts

HULL F.C.   SEASON 1895–1896
First team to play for Hull at The Boulevard,   v.   Liversedge, September 21st, 1895

Hull's team for the first match played at The Boulevard.

Back Row :   H. Hildreth (Hon. Joint Sec.,)   C. A. Brewer (President,)   G. Jacketts,   G. W. Stephenson (Hon. Joint Sec.)
Third Row :   H. Wiles,   W. Mansell,   W. Harmer,   J. S. Barker,   J. Townend,   G. Booth,   J. Gray (Attendant)
Second Row :   E. Mahoney,   H. Thompson,   C. C. Lempriere (Captain,)   C. Townend,   W. Johnson,   A. Plugge.   Front Row :   G. E. Barker,   W. Feetham,   J. Holmes

occasional break bringing relief to each side. Charlie Townend was prominent for Hull with a strong clearing run and Sharpe replied with a similar effort for Liversedge. Hull's forwards then produced a promising move with some short hand-to-hand passing, but it came to nothing. The home side were still attacking when the interval arrived with the crowd still awaiting the first points on the new ground.

They did not have too long to wait for it in the second half and the try by Jacketts raised hopes that Hull would pull clear. It was not to be, however, and the rest of the half continued to be a hard-fought battle with defences well on top. The nearest Hull came to scoring a second try came when they moved the ball swiftly from a scrum. Thornton punted the ball to Lempriere, who kicked ahead. A try looked imminent, but in the struggle to touch down Charlie Townend and Liversedge's Harry Barker collided with such impact that they had to go off for treatment for a while.

Liversedge's best effort thrilled the *Mail* reporter, who wrote: 'The spectators were then treated to a splendid series of passing, the ball being transferred between Wood, Jenkinson, Sharpe and Womersley with machine-like accuracy, the capital understanding between these players taking play from their own line to that of their opponents.'

Following the match a celebration dinner was held at the Imperial Hotel in Paragon Street attended by both teams and a host of other sporting celebrities. Mr C. A. Brewer, president, said: 'The Hull Club had started on a new venture. They had left the field which had been their home for many years and gone to another part of the town. In taking that action they had been severely criticised and had been told that they were going to lose money. As to whether they would be so unfortunate rested with the future.'

Hull: Johnson; Lempriere, Thompson, J. Townend, Mahoney; C. Townend, G. Barker; Wiles, J. Barker, Harmer, Mansell, Plugge, Holmes, Feetham, Jacketts.
Liversedge: R. Hallas; Jenkinson, B. Sharpe, J. Thornton, Womersley; H. Barker, R. Wood; G. Smith, Steele, N. Parkin, Sykes, S. Priestley, Medley, H. Ellis, Todkill.

Hull v. Hull Kingston Rovers

16 September 1899   League match
Craven Street, Hull

The most eagerly awaited event in the city's sporting history. That was the billing for the first Hull and Rovers derby under the auspices of the Northern Union. Although Hull had been founder members of the Northern Union in 1895, Rovers did not break away from the English Rugby Union until four years later. For years the supporters of each club had claimed their team was the best and thrown out unacceptable challenges. Now they were to meet in Rovers' first home match in the Northern Union. The rivalry between the two clubs had intensified since Hull had outbid and forced Rovers out of their Athletic Ground (later The Boulevard) home in 1895. This caused a sudden exchange of locality with Hull moving from east to west and Rovers going in the opposite direction. On a pleasant Saturday afternoon towards the end of the nineteenth century, the supporters of both clubs headed en-masse to Craven Street, off Holderness Road. A procession of wagonettes rolled over North Bridge with scores of policemen lining the route, ready to step in should the rival fans come to grips. In fact, the day passed without any great incident. One report even referred to a steady stream of non-smiling spectators, suggesting the serious faces were because 'the issue at stake was far too awful'. While Rovers were already known as the Robins or Redbreasts because of their jersey design, Hull had yet to acquire their famous irregular black and white hoops or Airlie Birds tag. Instead, their black jerseys earned them the nickname of the All Blacks, or Blackbirds.

Although the kick-off was not until 3.30 p.m. crowds began to gather outside the ground at noon, thirty minutes before the gates were due to be opened. It was reported that about twenty Rovers supporters had already been found inside the ground, having slept there overnight. Yet, for all that the match had been the talk of the city for weeks, the attendance of 12,000 to 14,000 was regarded as well below expectations although easily a ground record. The crowd estimate did not include the many spectators who gained a free view by clambering on to railway wagons left conveniently on the Northern Eastern line alongside the ground. Inside the ground there were a vast number of youths, but 'The gentler sex, of course, were not represented' according to one observer.

Each club had recruited from far a field and of the thirty players who trotted out for this momentous clash of local rivals only nine were born in the area, three in Hull's line-up and six in Rovers'. The Hull trio were Charles Lempriere, Billy Jacques and William Wiles. Although the Northern Union had already made significant rule changes to make the game more attractive, including the abolition of the lineout, it was still basically fifteen-a-side rugby union. Despite having played only two matches in the developing new code, Rovers were thought to have the edge in the forwards while Hull were known to be faster in the backs. The tight, little ground was thought to be an advantage to Rovers, but overall there was little to choose between the sides and betting was said to be evens.

Even more than a century ago, however, it was acknowledged that it is forwards who win matches, as observed by the *Hull Daily Mail* reporter following Rovers'

Hull 2   **Hull Kingston Rovers 8**
Drop goal: Jacques   *Tries:* Kemp, Starks
                                      Drop goal: Tulloch

HULL v. HULL KINGSTON ROVERS

The Hull Daily Mail comments in august language on the first Hull-Rovers derby match.

THE ROUT AT CRAVEN-STREET

HULL UPSET BY ROVERS.

That which has to be has been. Excitement generated and sustained by weeks of waiting, by calm confidence on the one side, and high hopes, and, as it once appeared, high presumption on the other, has waned, not, be it remarked for ever, but with strict reference to this first glorious and momentous struggle, the forerunner of many such.

It is well that between this event proper and its treatment there has been time for that calm reflection which tends to moderate the volume of triumph and, in less degree, to soothe wounded vanity and soften the bitterness of defeat. It is well, too, that the circumstances of the case admit of the exercise of that absolute impartiality with which the causes of a victory and a defeat must be weighed.

Ingrained in every Englishman is the sporting instinct, which moves him to wear his laurels with becoming modesty, to accept defeat with courage. So much is this part of the natural character that it is the commonplace of etiquette for the vanquished to be the first to salute his conqueror. That, I am sure do the Hull men, with all grace. When our sympathies become narrow and parochial, then may we for fear the well being of sport.

victory. He wrote: 'It may now be accepted as a general principle that a forward team with weak backs may hope to beat a back team, with not weak, but weaker forwards. The team which contains the weaker forwards must play whatever game its opponents dictate, which is generally a defensive game. The opportunity for aggression comes when the backs of the other team fail to respond to the calls of their own forwards.'

The supremacy of the home forwards became clear from the start as they surged downfield to score within a minute of Rovers forward Jack Rhodes kicking off. Hull failed to cover the kick properly and in the scramble for possession Anthony Starks emerged as the historic first scorer in a Humberside derby game. It was also Rovers' first Northern Union touchdown after two try-less matches. Starks made a mess of the conversion attempt.

Rovers continued to stick to their traditional game, bustling, rushing and tackling to such an extent that Hull rarely threatened the home line. An attack of nerves, a malady that was to strike them on numerous big match occasions in the years ahead, was already being blamed for Hull's failure to strike top form. 'It is strange that men with such wide experience as are to be found behind the Hull pack should be struck with stage fright. But they were, and at times their combined helplessness was appalling,' wrote one critic, adding: 'Hull's backs were never more than feebly aggressive.'

Considering Rovers' territorial advantage, Hull must have defended well to concede only one try until just before half-time when Albert Kemp forced his way over to make it 6-0. A drop goal by Jacques early in the second half edged Hull back into the game, which continued at a fast pace. Hull's backs began to show some improvement without being able to break clear of Rovers' tremendous defence and a home victory was sealed when Tulloch landed a late drop goal.

Hull: Sillis; Lempriere, Driscoll, Tanner, Jacques; Franks, Thompson; Cornish, Parkinson, Voyce, Rhodes, Gorman, Wiles, Dale, Fildes.

Hull K.R.: Sinclair; Tulloch, Ripton, Jackson, Ruddeforth; Guy, Levitt; Kemp, Starks, J. Rhodes, Fletcher, Stephenson, Noble, Debney, Windle.

HULL v. AUSTRALIA

30 January 1909   Tour match
The Boulevard, Hull

Hull have played the Australian tourists a dozen times and their only win came on the Kangaroos' first tour of 1908-9 after what was described as one of the most dramatic finishes ever seen at The Boulevard. The Airlie Birds were trailing 8-4 with only three minutes left and many fans, having given up hope, were already heading for the warmth of their homes on a bitterly cold Saturday afternoon.

Hull had done well enough in defence to restrict the Australians to two tries, but they had rarely threatened the opposition line themselves and in the gathering gloom there seemed little prospect of a late breakthrough. Then came the sudden change from depression to delight, characterised by the *Hull Daily Mail's* story of a fan.

'I heard a story of a disappointed supporter who had left The Boulevard in a fit of depression and on reaching Airlie Street there arose that vociferous cheer, which proclaimed Holder's try,' wrote 'Athleo'. 'Speedily he returned to learn the joyful tidings and beheld a sight he had hardly dare gaze upon. Rogers was in the act of placing the ball for the kick and in his fear and trembling that the local player would fail, the excited prodigal remained at the back of the East stand to await the verdict of the crowd. It is really funny how some people will be carried away by their excitement. I can readily excuse the victim on this memorable occasion, for not only were the ladies in the "Official stall" just below the Press stand so frightened that they could not speak, but amid the weather-beaten and veteran followers of rugby football around me a deathly silence prevailed as Rogers brought the ball back.

'The home record had been severely tried [Hull had not lost at The Boulevard that season], and in the fleeting moment we anxiously awaited the reprieve or death sentence. Nothing short of a cyclone could have diverted the ball from its speedy passage over the cross bar, and while on its journey the joyous shouts which rent the air were sufficient to frighten the gods and one telephone operator at the *Mail*.'

Ned Rogers' winning goal was from a fairly simple position, although the pressure he was under must have been immense. The try by Bill Holder, however, deserved to win any match. The big forward did not score many tries, only 30 in almost 300 appearances for Hull, but this was one to treasure and was talked about long after the event. A former Gloucester Rugby Union player, Holder was in his second season with Hull after making remarkable progress in the first year when he played for Great Britain against New Zealand. Holder enjoyed the more running opportunities he received in the thirteen-a-side game and revealed pace, power and mobility to break through in for his memorable try.

The match against Hull was the Kangaroos' thirty-fourth of the tour and over familiarity with the tourists was given as a reason for a 'disappointing' attendance of 10,000 and £268 receipts. In fact, only the tour matches at Leeds, Oldham and Broughton Rangers attracted bigger club crowds. The Kangaroos' star attraction was the legendary Dally Messenger, who had also toured with the first New Zealand squad a year earlier. Regarded as one of the all-time great centres, Messenger was on the wing against Hull and apart from kicking a goal did not make a great impact at The Boulevard.

Hull 9
  Try: Holder
  Goals: E. Rogers (3)

Australia 8
  Tries: Rosenfeld, Courtney
  Goal: Messenger

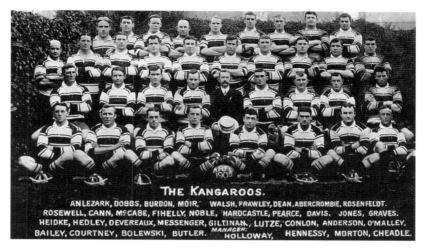

THE KANGAROOS.

ANLEZARK, DOBBS, BURDON, MOIR. WALSH, FRAWLEY, DEAN, ABERCROMBIE, ROSENFELDT.
ROSEWELL, CANN, McCABE, FIHELLY, NOBLE, HARDCASTLE, PEARCE, DAVIS. JONES, GRAVES.
HEIDKE, HEDLEY, DEVEREAUX, MESSENGER, GILTINAN., LUTZE, CONLON, ANDERSON, O'MALLEY,
BAILEY, COURTNEY, BOLEWSKI, BUTLER. *MANAGER:* HOLLOWAY, HENNESSY, MORTON, CHEADLE.

The full 1908-09 Australia tour squad.

There was a more impressive display by Albert Rosenfeld, who was to join Huddersfield and score a record eighty tries in a season. Although he was to earn his place in the Rugby Football League's Hall of Fame as a winger, Rosenfeld was a stand off and virtually unknown in England when he arrived with the Kangaroos. He stood out at half-back against Hull with his dodging runs, which made him a constant threat and brought him one of Australia's two tries.

There was also a top-class performance by centre Jimmy Devereux, who along with his wing partner Andy Morton, became the first of many Australians to sign for Hull. Although Morton did not stay long, Devereux made 180 appearances and became a great favourite with The Boulevard crowd.

Rosenfeld's try and one from Tedda Courtney, plus Messenger's goal was a fair reflection of the game going into the closing stages. Only two penalty goals by Ned Rogers had kept Hull in touch and even after their eventual victory the general view was that the tourists had been unlucky. But co-manager Jack Fihelly had high praise for Hull's international full-back Harry Taylor and half-back Bill Anderson, saying he had not seen two more brilliant players and that the home side owed their victory to them.

The match was described as an outstanding example of how the new code of rugby was developing. It was only two years since the reduction of teams to thirteen players and the introduction of the play-the-ball, to make it now quite distinctive from Rugby Union. One report said: 'The Northern Union code, with its large range of possibilities has repeatedly afforded instances of where one team, by displaying the essence of courage and tenacity has snatched victory when their chances had well nigh sunk to zero. Saturday's was such a game.'

Hull: Taylor; E. Rogers, G. Rogers, Cotterill, Dechan; Jones, Anderson; Herridge, Holder, Boylen, Stevenson, Walton, Major.
Australia: Hedley; Messenger, Heidke, Devereux, Morton; Rosenfeld, Anlezark; Graves, O'Malley, Abercrombie, Courtney, Hardcastle, Moir.

HULL v. WAKEFIELD TRINITY

18 April 1914
Thrum Hall, Halifax

Northern Union (Rugby League) Challenge
Cup final

The most momentous match in Hull's long history? This winning of the Northern Union Challenge Cup must be the one. It was the first trophy won by the club since the 1895 breakaway and ended a run of several bitter disappointments, including three successive NU Cup final defeats a few years earlier.

Although Hull were hot favourites to beat a Wakefield Trinity side that had finished seventeenth in the League table, the final whistle was greeted with relief and then unprecedented scenes of jubilation by their army of fans. The relief came because fourth-placed Hull had to battle much harder than expected, with both of their two tries not coming until the last five minutes. Trinity also won high praise for pushing Hull all the way despite being reduced to twelve men in the forty-fifth minute following the dismissal of second row forward and captain Herbert Kershaw for kicking Hull winger Alf Francis. In fact, Wakefield finished with only eleven players as Tommy Poynton went off injured just before Hull scored their second try.

But though the Wakefield underdogs gained much sympathy and were thought to be unlucky by many, Hull considered they were worthy winners of the Cup after having beaten the holders Huddersfield in the semi-final. Huddersfield's famous team of 'All the Talents' were sweeping all before them at the time, and Hull's victory was a terrific morale-booster. The club had built their own team of stars with a number of Australians plus the sensational signing of Billy Batten from Hunslet a year earlier for a then record £600, twice the previous highest transfer fee.

The powerful international centre transformed Hull from a good team who had never won anything to a great side who carried off all the trophies in the next few seasons, starting with the Northern Union Cup. It was Batten alone, argued Wakefield followers, who beat them in the 1914 final. The *Yorkshire Post* went some way to agreeing with that view with their correspondent writing: 'Batten was in magnificent form both in defence and attack all through the piece. His whirlwind rushes always raised the excitement of the crowd to a high pitch, and how some of those rushes were stopped was high tribute to the merit of the Trinity tacklers. Though Batten did not score himself, he deserves most of the credit for the first try. He was the life and soul of the Hull attack, and he was always a stalwart in defence, saving his line on several occasions.'

The *Hull Daily Mail* was equally certain about Batten's contribution to victory. 'Without the slightest hesitation I say Batten won Hull the coveted victory,' wrote Orion. 'The master mind was ever working. He feared no foe as he dashed through with those telling bursts, demonstrating no respect for Wakefield. Batten was on the field to win by a combination of Yorkshire-born flesh and blood and the grit of a collier. He was up against quite a number of men of his own type, who 'spotted' him whenever possible. The only difference was that he was more enterprising and dashing than they. Batten knew the best way to win – not by booting the ball and tackling, as Wakefield generally resorted to, or missing

---

Hull 6
Tries: Harrison, Francis

Wakefield Trinity 0

chances of scoring through nerves or ill-judged runs into the arms of opponents. Wakefield sportsmen blame Batten for Hull winning the Cup. I quite agree with them.'

Batten formed a powerful centre partnership with Bert Gilbert, who had been signed after starring for Australia on the Kangaroo's recent tour. Gilbert was appointed captain and thus became the first Australian to lead a side to victory in a Challenge Cup final.

Hull's victory came only three months before the outbreak of the First World War and their vital first try was scored by Jack Harrison, who was to be killed in action three years later and become Rugby League's only winner of the Victoria Cross for bravery.

Wakefield, who had won only twelve of their thirty-four League matches, were mostly a team of solid performers who had upset the form book by reaching the final. At half back they had Jonty Parkin, then a nineteen-year-old inexperienced youth who was to become one of the game's greatest players.

A glance at the two line-ups made it clear why Hull were such overwhelming favourites, with many of their supporters snapping up odds of 1-5 on a black and white victory. The final came towards the end of a hectic programme of fixtures for both clubs, Hull playing their ninth match in twenty-eight days. But Hull had banked all on winning the Cup and five days before the final they fielded a side against Swinton including only two of their final team. Two days after winning the Cup they lost at Huddersfield in a championship semi-final. With Great Britain to tour Australia that summer it was decided to split the departing squads in two, allowing players involved in the Cup and championship finals to follow later. In fact, Hull's Francis was the only tourist to play in the Challenge Cup final.

It was estimated that half of the 19,000 crowd packed into the tight Thrum Hall ground were from Hull and they certainly made most of the pre-match noise. They were quieter early in the game as Wakefield went near to scoring a quick try and two of their drop goal attempts went wide. Hull gradually powered their way into the game without being able to dominate as expected and a hard-fought first half ended without a score after Wakefield failed with a kick from a now long-extinct mark. Wakefield might have given Hull more trouble but they wasted much of their possession by kicking too much, which allowed the Airlie Birds to grind their way back and put the opposition under pressure. The forward battle became intense with every one of Hull's pack earning high praise for refusing to take a backward step and gradually they began to get on top. Steve Darmody at loose forward was picked out for extra mention as he revelled in the fierce exchanges and set a tremendous hard-working lead. Behind Hull's pack, scrum-half Billy Anderson provided the perfect link with his threequarters, even in the second half when an ankle caused him much pain.

Batten continued to be the biggest threat to Wakefield and only a last ditch tackle stopped him scoring an early second half try after beating several players on a typical rampaging run. Then came the dismissal of Kershaw by St Helens referee

---

Hull: E. Rogers; Francis, Gilbert, Batten, Harrison; Devereux, Anderson; Herridge, Holder, Dick Taylor, Hammill, Grice, Darmody.

Wakefield T: Land; Johnson, Lynch, Poynton, Howarth; J. Parkin, Millican; Dixon, Crosland, E. Parkin, Kershaw, Beattie, Burton.

Hull v. Wakefield Trinity

Bert Gilbert, Hull's Cup final captain.

James May, who had consulted a touch judge, and after an immediate gallant response by the remaining Trinity dozen Hull finally began to get on top. It seemed they had made the vital breakthrough midway through the half when a wayward Wakefield kick resulted in Harrison and Gilbert breaking away only for a forward pass to spoil the chances of a first try.

Wakefield continued to show dogged resistance and it was not until the last five minutes that Hull scored the only points of the match. Almost inevitably it was Batten who finally broke Trinity's resistance. Receiving an inside pass from Harrison, the big centre thundered past several defenders before returning the ball to his winger who went in for the vital touchdown. Hull fans erupted, sounding hand bells and bugles in a deafening cacophony of noise. There were also choruses of '2, 4, 7, 9, 11', which was the sequence of scoring in Hull's 11-3 surprise semi-final defeat of Huddersfield. Ned Rogers' missed goal kick did nothing to quieten the ecstatic supporters and it is said Hull's last minute try went almost unnoticed as they were still celebrating the first score.

Those who were still watching the game saw another well-executed move that ended with Gilbert sending in Alf Francis on the other wing. Rogers again failed with the goal kick, which was followed by the final whistle and an immediate invasion of the pitch by hordes of Hull fans. A battered Batten, who had been carried off injured just before the last try, was given a special cheer but all the players were hailed as heroes.

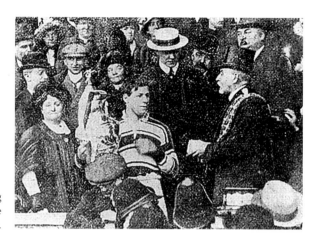

An 1914 newspaper cutting showing Bert Gilbert receiving the Cup from the Mayor of Halifax.

The Mayor of Halifax presented Gilbert with the coveted trophy before Hull set off home by train. They got off at North Ferriby and transferred to a charabanc to make the last eight miles of their journey by road with huge crowds welcoming them along the way. Back in Hull, the team were paraded on the City Hall balcony and the Mayor ended his speech of appreciation with the hope that it would not be long before they won the Cup again. In fact, it was be another sixty-eight years.

HULL v. HUDDERSFIELD

24 April 1920   Championship final
Headingley, Leeds

Best in the Northern Union! Twenty-five years after the historic breakaway from the English Rugby Union, Hull won the championship for the first time. But they were never given full credit for lifting the title as Huddersfield had finished seven points clear of second-placed Hull and were then deprived of five players, who were on the way to Australia with the Great Britain tour squad, when they met in the championship final. Huddersfield, who were aiming to achieve the 'All Four Cups' feat for a second time, were also without injured Test winger Stan Moorhouse.

What is often ignored is that Hull were also under full strength and played more than half the game with only twelve men after Alf Grice was sent off just before half-time. Although Billy Stone was their only Great Britain tourist, injuries and suspension robbed Hull of other first team players including Ned Rogers, who went on to play in a club record 500 matches.

Huddersfield's belief that they had been dealt an unfair hand in having to contest the final without five tourists, including their great captain Harold Wagstaff, was given added poignancy when Billy Batten scored Hull's late match-winning try. The legendary centre had turned down the chance of a tour place when he refused to play in a trial match and was not considered for the squad.

'To Batten went the distinction of pulling the game out of the fire,' said one report. 'He had just previously missed by an arm's length a try which a great dribble by Kennedy had made possible. Batten, in his eagerness to support, kicked a trifle too hard and the ball rolled dead. But Hull would, indeed, have been unlucky had not Batten achieved his object a little later with a flying leap near the corner flag. It was a near thing, but Batten, with characteristic boldness, made it a certainty. Huddersfield's centres, Gleeson and Rosenfeld, stuck well to Batten for most of the game but their combined attentions could not quite subdue the Hull giant.'

With so many star players missing from both teams the game failed to rise above the mediocre and was marred by a succession of penalties, fourteen in as many minutes from the kick-off and totalling well over thirty by the finish. They were mostly for technical offences and the dismissal of Grice in the thirty-seventh minute was for a rare foul. In fact, one of the few injuries during the game was sustained by the referee, Mr. Hestford, who was laid out after coming into contact with a late rampaging Hull attack.

Despite snatching victory by only one point, the general view was that Hull fully deserved to win. Both teams were criticised for one what one reporter described as 'simply a distortion of the finer arts of the code'. It was only in the last twenty minutes that Hull began to move the ball about and attack with their usual flair, so that despite being a man short they began to outplay their opponents.

Hull had reached the final with an 11-0 home defeat of Leeds, while Huddersfield had scraped through with a 7-5 defeat of Widnes. The play offs to decide the championship were necessary because the clubs had different fixtures and did not play the same number of matches. There is no doubt Huddersfield were regarded as, not only the best team of the season but also one of the greatest of all

---

Hull 3   **Huddersfield 2**
Try: Batten   *Goal:* Holland

Hull's 1920 Championship-winning team. *From left to right, back row* : Jack Beasty, Jimmy Devereux, Tom Herridge, Eddie Caswell, Fred Newsome, Percy Oldham, Jim Humphries. *Third row*: Danny Wyburn, Harold Garrett, Bob Taylor, Eddie Shields, Alf Grice, Billy Holder, Sid Melville (trainer). *Sitting*: A.J. Boynton (chairman), Jack Holdsworth, Billy Batten, Jim Kennedy, Tommy Milner, Steve Markham, C.N. Lofthouse (secretary). *Front*: Alf Francis, Jack Hulme.

time. Known as 'The Team of all Talents', they had won all the four cups in 1914-15 before competitive rugby was suspended for the duration of the First World War, and needed only to beat Hull to retain them all.

They had held on to the Northern Union Challenge Cup by winning the final two weeks earlier when they had all their tourists available. A crowd of 12,900 greeted the teams when they took the field on a bright afternoon that still left the pitch on the heavy side following earlier rain. Huddersfield had brought the Northern Union Cup with them and it was prominently displayed in the main stand. Expectations of a free-flowing game were soon dispelled as a scrum followed the kick-off, and that resulted in the first of many penalties. It was stop-start for most of the first quarter, only relieved by a powerful run by Batten which came to nothing when Bob Taylor failed to take his pass.

Batten continued to be prominent, but his over eagerness led to Huddersfield taking the lead in the twenty-seventh minute when he was spotted offside and Major Holland landed the penalty. Worse was to follow for Hull as Grice's dismissal came after thirty-seven minutes and a 2-0 deficit at the interval looked ominous. The penalties continued to flow in the second half and Holland was off target with an early attempt before Jim Kennedy twice failed to equalise, hitting a post with one shot.

As rain began to fall, Hull's victory hopes looked as if they were going to be washed away until a change of tactics and more adventurous play began to take effect. It finally paid off with Batten's mighty solo effort and Kennedy received a tremendous ovation from Hull fans when he hoisted the trophy aloft.

Hull: Holdsworth; Francis, Batten, Kennedy, Markham; Milner, Hulme; Grice, Holder, Shields, Bob Taylor, Garrett, Wyburn.

Huddersfield: Holland; Todd, Rosenfeld, Gleeson, Pogson; Marsden, Habron; Swinden, Naylor, Higson, Fenwick, Sherwood, Sutcliffe.

HULL v. HULL KINGSTON ROVERS

27 November 1920   Yorkshire Cup final
Headingley, Leeds

This was the first time Hull and Rovers had met in any final and it produced one of the most dramatic finishes involving the two arch rivals. The grim, muddy battle on a miserably wet November afternoon seemed to be heading for a pointless draw when Rovers winger Billy Bradshaw snatched victory with an amazing 40-yard drop goal.

This is how the *Hull Daily Mail* reported the most famous single score in derby history: 'With no score one minute from time the majority anticipated a drawn game, but one of those things which rarely happen came into this game and gave Rovers victory. Kennedy mis-fielded the ball in his own half and it was this that gave the Robins their chance. From the scrimmage their backs passed well and McGiever kicked up in front of Hulls posts. Ned Rogers fielded and preferred to kick instead of running until he was tackled. He had the mortification of seeing the ball drop into the hands of Bradshaw. There was no one near Bradshaw, and this player just getting into position steadied himself and took the fate of the club in his hands by attempting to drop a goal. He succeeded!

'Had he failed, he would probably have been blamed for not trying to get over the line. As the score happened in the last two or three minutes of the game there was no chance for Hull to overhaul it and the cheering for the points had not died down when referee Hestford blew his whistle for time.'

Sixty years later Frank Bielby, Rovers' tough-tackling forward, was still convinced Bradshaw could have scored a match-winning try. In an interview shortly before the famous Hull-Rovers Wembley final of 1980 he told me: 'When Rogers fielded the ball under his own posts I followed up and forced him to kick-off his wrong foot and instead of going downfield the ball flew off his boot right into Bradshaw's hands about 40 yards away. I can see him now. He was a fast winger and all he had to do was run for the corner. There was nobody to stop him apart from Rogers and he was slugged. Instead he took a million to one chance. First he wiped the ball down his jersey and then sent it soaring to the posts with a drop kick. I watched the ball going up and thought what a waste. It seemed the ball was never going to come down, but it did just between the posts. Well, Bradshaw was the hero then and we all rushed to shake his hand.'

The goal was a stunning blow to Hull, who had not lost to Rovers in peace time since Boxing Day 1913 – a run of eight unbeaten matches, including a draw. Their latest victory had been 15-6 at home less than two months earlier. Although both clubs had tried to have the final staged at a more local venue there was still a mass exodus from the city's two railway stations, Paragon and Cannon Street. Hopes of a record crowd faded with the dismal weather, however, and about 20,000 greeted the two teams with Hull's fans providing the loudest support. Rovers fielded ten local-born players against Hull's four.

The heavy conditions, with rain continuing during the game, were expected to favour Hull, who fielded a very big pack in the hope of winning the scrums to provide plenty of possession for an impressive back line that included the great Billy

---

Hull 0   **Hull Kingston Rovers 2**
                    Drop goal: Bradshaw

ROVERS WILL BRING HOME THE CUP
2-0

THE GREAT FOOTBALL FESTIVAL AT HEADINGLEY

MURKY SKIES AND MORNING RAIN DO NOT DETER RIVAL SUPPORTERS

LEEDS STREETS RING WITH BELLS AND RATTLES, AND FLASH WITH FAVOURS

SCORELESS AND STUBBORN FIRST HALF IN THE MUD

BRADSHAW'S BEAUTIFUL CUP-WINNING GOAL 3 MINUTES FROM TIME

How the *Hull Daily Mail* headlined their Yorkshire Cup final report.

Batten. But Rovers' hooker Sandy Gibson upset those plans by winning the scrums at an alarming rate even when Bielby was withdrawn from the pack to bolster their back division's defence. When Hull did have possession they squandered it with too much kicking, so things looked ominous when the first half ended scoreless despite the Airlie Birds having had the wind behind them.

They had gone nearest to scoring a try just before the interval when Billy Stone broke away down the wing. When the cover came across the winger kicked inside towards the line and speedy forward Bob Taylor won the chase to reach the ball but not before it had just gone dead. Alf Francis also went close when he was flung into touch near the corner after strong play from Batten.

Rovers had rarely threatened to score a try and Bradshaw, who was to be cheered off following his late match-winning drop goal, provoked early groans after missing with an early penalty shot close to the posts. Although the exchanges were always fierce the match did not gain the notoriety of some derby clashes after the referee gave a first half warning to both teams. Later he had to caution Bob Taylor and Gibson when they came to blows.

The second half followed a similar pattern to the first with Hull twice going within inches of scoring a try and Batten being brought down after beating several players on a typical 50-yard charge. Tenacious tackling foiled many other efforts with Arthur Moore setting a great example as Rovers' captain. As darkness descended, making it difficult to follow play from the Press box, most Rovers fans would have happily settled for a draw. Indeed, some had already departed to catch an early train when they must have been stopped in their tracks by the mighty roar that greeted Bradshaw's astonishing match-winning goal.

Hull: E. Rogers; Francis, Stone, Batten, Holdsworth; Milner, Caswell; Beasty, Hewson, H. Taylor, Bob Taylor, Wyburn, Kennedy.

Hull K.R.: Osborne; Harris, Austin, Cook, Bradshaw; McGiever, Clark; J.H. Wilkinson, R. Boagey, J.R. Wilkinson, Bielby, Gibson, Moore.

HULL v. HULL KINGSTON ROVERS

Sweet revenge! Five months after losing 2-0 to Rovers in the Yorkshire Cup final, Hull beat their deadly rivals by the same margin to lift a much bigger prize. The clubs were then the two major powers with Rovers finishing top and Hull a close-run second. Hull were defending champions and seeking to become only the third club to take the title in successive seasons.

A close game was expected, but Hull seemed to be heading for a comfortable victory after an hour when they led 14-4, having scored four tries to none. Then Rovers came storming back and a game that had lacked any real excitement because of Hull's clear superiority suddenly burst into pulsating life. It was all Rovers in the last twenty minutes and the many neutrals in the ground got behind them as they went all out for an unlikely victory. With just over a minute left the score was 16-11 when Cook flashed through and touched down near enough to the posts to give Sandy Gibson the chance to kick what looked like a simple equalising conversion. He had already kicked four goals, but the occasion proved too much for him and he pushed it wide. Five months earlier Billy Bradshaw's last minute Yorkshire Cup final winning goal had sent Rovers supporters wild with delight and now it was a Rovers miss that had Hull fans dancing a victory jig.

Although Rovers received due acclaim for their fight-back, most reports acknowledged that Hull were much the better team for most of the game and fully deserved to retain the title. Among several impressive individuals, Hull forward Danny Wyburn was hailed as the real hero after leaving the field at half-time nursing a badly gashed head. He did not immediately resume in the second half, but re-appeared a little later with his head swathed in bandage to continue his outstanding contribution to victory.

Wyburn and Bob Taylor formed a formidable second row and the pair combined in great style for the latter to score the second of his two tries. One report described it as an 'epic' touchdown and typical of Taylor, whose thirty-six tries in 1925-26 was to remain a record for a forward for forty-five years. Wyburn set up the try after fielding a loose ball and charging forward before unleashing Taylor on a 35-yard gallop to the posts.

To complete an outstanding back three, there was also an impressive performance by Harold Garrett at loose forward. With the front row winning a monopoly of possession from the scrums, Hull's forwards certainly overturned their reputation as probably the most criticised pack in the game. Their domination of the Rovers pack also allowed half-backs Tommy Milner and Eddie Caswell to dictate matters in midfield, with the latter particularly outstanding. Although Rovers did a good job keeping Billy Batten in check for most of the game, Hull's great centre ran strongly to set up Billy Stone's try.

One major disappointment was a crowd of only 10,000, which was half that who saw the teams contest the Yorkshire Cup final at the same ground earlier in the season. A major coal strike had limited travel by train and it was reckoned only 600 fans made the trip from Hull with the majority wearing Rovers colours. Some efforts

---

Hull 16
Tries: Taylor (2), Devereux, Stone
Goals: Kennedy (2)

Hull Kingston Rovers 14
Tries: Cook, Mulvey
Goals: Gibson (4)

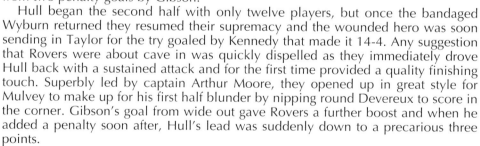

The great Billy Batten, who played a major role in Hull's championship success.

had been made to switch the match to Hull City's ground, but they came to nothing.

Hull's 9-4 interval lead did not reflect their first half supremacy as they scored three tries to nil without being able to add a single goal, Jim Kennedy's best effort hitting a post and bouncing out. The tries by Jimmy Devereux, Stone and Taylor were all well taken and there would have been more but for Rovers ending other promising attacks with last-ditch tackling. Devereux twice went near to touching down before the winger found himself with a clear run in.

Rovers poor finishing spoiled some good approach work with their most blatant miss being when Mulvey appeared to have a clear run in and inexplicably threw the ball behind him and Hull's Taylor gratefully kicked it into touch. It was a terrible error by the winger and Rovers' only first half points came from two penalty goals by Gibson.

Hull began the second half with only twelve players, but once the bandaged Wyburn returned they resumed their supremacy and the wounded hero was soon sending in Taylor for the try goaled by Kennedy that made it 14-4. Any suggestion that Rovers were about cave in was quickly dispelled as they immediately drove Hull back with a sustained attack and for the first time provided a quality finishing touch. Superbly led by captain Arthur Moore, they opened up in great style for Mulvey to make up for his first half blunder by nipping round Devereux to score in the corner. Gibson's goal from wide out gave Rovers a further boost and when he added a penalty soon after, Hull's lead was suddenly down to a precarious three points.

Kennedy eased Hull's anxiety with his a penalty, but Rovers were now playing much the better rugby and an all-out attack in the closing stages ended with Cook racing in for the try that gave them a great chance of forcing a replay. But Gibson could not land the goal.

Hull: E. Rogers; Devereux, Kennedy, Batten, Stone; Milner, Caswell; Beasty, Ellis, Newsome, Wyburn, Bob Taylor, Garrett.

Hull K.R.: Osborne; Harris, Austin, Cook, Mulvey; Clark, McGiever; J.H. Wilkinson, J.R. Wilkinson, Bielby, R. Boagey, A. Moore, Gibson.

HULL v. ROCHDALE HORNETS

29 April 1922
Headingley, Leeds

Northern Union (Rugby League) Challenge
Cup final

Hull have suffered many Challenge Cup final disappointments, but this was probably the unluckiest defeat of all. It was hailed as the greatest ever final at the time with Hull playing magnificently to outscore Rochdale by three tries to two. The day was packed with incident as hundreds of the record 32,596 crowd spilled on to the pitch after a barricade collapsed and had to be kept back by mounted policemen. The legendary Hull centre Billy Batten scored one of his famous leaping tries, while forward colleague Edgar Morgan was controversially denied a try when he was adjudged to have stepped into touch. Hull's luck seemed to be out from the start as, after Jim Kennedy had opened the scoring with an early try, his kick from near touch hit the crossbar. That was to prove the costliest of near misses, although captain Billy Stone was also off-target when he took over the goal kicking and attempted to add a match-winning conversion after Bob Taylor scored a magnificent late try.

Batten was again a tremendous force for Hull and his try was even highlighted by the *Rochdale Observer,* whose correspondent wrote: 'Stone sped down the touchline, and although held by Fitton, threw the ball inside to Batten, who was then about ten yards from the line. As Prescott crouched low to tackle, Batten made a wonderful leap over his back, and before he could be prevented he flung out his arms and just planted the ball over the line near the corner. It was a wonderful effort but Batten appeared to be in touch when he dropped over Prescott's back, and the Hornets' players were inclined to dispute the award of the try, which was given after Mr. Jones [referee] had consulted the touch judge.'

The decision to award the try was one of the few that went Hull's way, with the disallowing of Morgan's effort being the most contentious. Brilliant play by Kennedy following an interception had given the former Wales Rugby Union international forward the chance and he flung himself over in the corner to the wild acclaim of Hull fans. But the cheers turned to groans when the referee consulted the near touch judge, who ruled Morgan had stepped into touch. It must have been only by the width of a blade of grass, and one report suggested it was difficult to judge because spectators and a mounted policeman were almost on the pitch in that corner. In contrast, Hull's objections to Fitton's second try for Rochdale went unheeded. Overall there is no doubt that Hull were extremely unlucky to lose, but credit must be given to Rochdale and particularly their forwards for a supreme effort. It is said that Rochdale forwards won the match because they dominated the scrums 'with every member of their pack pushing their full weight'.

Even before the kick-off the crowd scenes were such as have never been seen at the famous ground before or since. Headingley was already full to heaving when a delayed train load of Rochdale fans arrived just as the teams were coming out. By then there were about 1,000 spectators waiting to gain entrance and when they threatened to rush the gates, orders were given to open them. The fans then poured in without paying and did not contribute to the record receipts of £2,964. Other

---

Hull 9
Tries: Batten, Kennedy, Taylor

Rochdale Hornets 10
Tries: Fitton (2)
Goals: Paddon (2)

Hull's 1922 Northern Union Challenge Cup final squad. *From left to right, back row* : Danny Wyburn, Jack Beasty, Bob Taylor, Edgar Morgan, George Oliver, Billy Charles, Joe Ellis (did not play). *Sitting*: Harold Garratt, Ned Rogers (did not play), Billy Batten, Billy Stone, Jim Kennedy, Jack Holdsworth, Sid Melville (trainer). *Front*: Eddie Caswell, Emlyn Gwynne.

non-paying fans viewed the match while clinging to trees and telegraph poles at what is now the scoreboard end.

It was estimated that 7,000 Hull fans made the trip at what one report said was a considerable sacrifice as the nation was in a deep financial depression at the time. But all were in good heart as they fully expected their heroes to bring home the Cup they had last won eight years earlier. The programme notes reflected their confidence, stating that Hull were popular favourites due mainly to Rochdale's backs being much weaker than Batten and company. Third-placed Hull had finished four places above Rochdale and been beaten 27-8 at Wigan in the championship play-off semi-final a week earlier. After playing nine matches in twenty-one days, the week's rest was said to have left Hull in splendid condition and they were at full strength apart from the absence of injured Ned Rogers, their long-serving full-back.

Hull: Holdsworth; Gwynne, Kennedy, Batten, Stone; Charles, Caswell; Beasty, Oliver, Morgan, Wyburn, Bob Taylor, Garratt.

Rochdale H.: Prescott; Fitton, Wild, McLoughlin, Joe Corsi; Heaton, Kynan; Woods, Bennett, Harris, Paddon, Edwards, L. Corsi.

HULL v. ROCHDALE HORNETS

The match was the last to be played under the old Northern Union title before it became the Rugby Football League. It was also to be Rochdale's only Challenge Cup final appearance and is still regarded as the greatest day in the club's long history. The first sign that luck would not favour Hull came when they lost the toss and began the game facing wind and sun. But that seemed a minor setback when Hull shot into the lead within eight minutes, following enterprising play by Kennedy, who charged down Jack Heaton's kick and just managed to win the race to touch down before the ball ran dead. Kennedy's conversion attempt hit the crossbar and bounced out. Little did anyone realise that was to prove a crucial miss in the final analysis. A few minutes later Rochdale's Dicky Paddon landed a penalty goal from a similarly difficult position and added another with a great shot to put Hornets ahead after eighteen minutes following Jack Beasty's foul on Eddie McLoughlin, who was breaking through.

Two minutes later Rochdale surged further ahead with an excellent try by Fitton. Louis Corsi made the initial break and did well to get the ball away when tackled for Fitton to dodge past Stone and Batten for the touchdown. The game continued at a cracking pace and Hull hit back with Batten's try to be only a point behind after half an hour. Just before half-time there was a scramble near the Hull line and Dicky Kynan claimed a try. The referee said 'no' and it remained 7-6 to Rochdale at the interval.

There were further crowd problems before the teams came out again with more barricades crumbling and the second half began with almost as much happening off the field as on it. The disallowing of Morgan's touchdown added to the tension and then came Fitton's second try that sent Rochdale's fans wild. It followed a scrum

Harold Garratt, a forward stalwart in Hull's 1922 Cup final pack.

Emlyn Gwynne, on the losing side in two successive NU Challenge Cup finals after switching from Rugby Union.

near to Hull's line and the ball was whipped out to Fitton, the winger slipping round Kennedy before diving over in the corner. Paddon failed with the conversion after being hampered by a spectator, who he had to forcibly remove from the touchline.

It was now 10-6 to Rochdale with seventeen minutes left and one report described the crowd as being in a frenzied state of excitement. It became 'white hot' a few moments later when Hull forwards Morgan and Taylor charged down field and from the position gained the latter blasted through a massed defence for a tremendous solo try in the seventieth minute. Stone missed with the kick, but it still looked as if Hull were about to snatch victory and would have done so had Rochdale not reached great heights in defence to hold out against a wave of attacks.

Hull's fans were stunned into silence at the finish, but a large crowd awaited the team's return and they were given a victor's welcome home.

HULL v. HUDDERSFIELD

24 November 1923
Headingley, Leeds

Yorkshire Cup final

Eighteen years after the competition was launched and in their fourth county final, Hull at last lifted the Yorkshire Cup. Victory completed their haul of all four major trophies and came just in time before the remaining few of their first great team retired or departed. It was to be thirteen years before Hull won another trophy.

Huddersfield were also coming to the end of a glorious era for the club and the twilight clash of the Titans was personified in the centre duel between two of the game's most legendary players. Billy Batten, the idol of The Boulevard for ten years, was now thirty-four, while opposite him the Prince of centres, Harold Wagstaff, was thirty-two. King Billy was in his final season for Hull and he produced a vintage performance that included his last try for the Airlie Birds. He was also involved in Hull's other try and still had the power to bring off the trademark smothering tackles that shattered opponents before they could get into full stride.

Batten was one of only two players to collect all four major Cup-winning medals with Hull during that era, the other being long-serving Ned Rogers. Both had played in the 1914 Northern Union Cup final and Rogers also dug deep to give a reminder of his best days as he helped Hull to their first Yorkshire Cup success. The little full-back, who was coming to the end of his club record – nineteen years at Hull – suffered a bad knock late on when he was laid out by a high tackle after passing the ball. Rogers had plenty to smile about when he went up for his winner's medal as the only player to have played in all three of Hull's losing county finals.

While two of Hull's greatest and most popular players were coming to the end of their careers, the 1923 Yorkshire Cup final confirmed the emergence of another who was to become a Boulevard legend. Joe Oliver began his long career at Huddersfield and the youngster's appearance in the final was opposite Hull. It was only his eleventh senior game since being signed from Cumberland amateur rugby earlier in the year and he displayed much of the attributes that were to lead to Great Britain honours. Playing at full-back, Oliver showed no signs of nerves despite the electric atmosphere and early in the first half landed a mighty drop goal after fielding a clearance kick by Rogers. Oliver joined Hull five years later and went on to score club records of 687 goals and 1,842 points.

Despite their fading glories, both teams still commanded loyal support and the crowd of 23,300 was one of the biggest to attend a county final. The weather was unusually perfect for a November afternoon with the sun shining gloriously, no wind and the pitch in excellent condition after being covered overnight to beat the threat of frost. Hull lost the toss and were given quite a first half handicap in having to face the dazzling sun. Slightly against the run of play Ben Gronow put Huddersfield in front with a splendid penalty goal after five minutes and went further ahead in the tenth minute with Oliver's mighty drop goal. After a period of hard-fought midfield play Hull suddenly opened up in the twenty-fifth minute to score a marvellous try. Stan Whitty was the instigator when he broke away from the centre and after slipping past one defender handed on to Batten, who quickly transferred to Collins. The ball was then flashed to Jim Kennedy, who hit top speed to go over too far out for him to add the goal.

Hull 10
Tries: Batten, Kennedy
Goals: Kennedy (2)

Huddersfield 4
Goal: Gronow
Drop goal: Oliver

Captain Edgar Morgan carries off the Yorkshire Cup followed by the rest of the Hull forwards: Harold Garrett, Bob Taylor, Bill Brennan, Harold Bowman, Jack Beasty. (Drawn by cartoonist Ern Shaw.)

Although Hull produced other superb first-half attacks, the Huddersfield defence rose to the task and they held out to take a 4-3 interval lead. Both teams seemed to rely on what one report described as 'monotonous kicking'. Even Batten did not escape the criticism. 'I cannot understand why Batten departed from his old theory on one occasion when he applied a long raking kick instead of entrusting the ball to Collins, who was so well placed to give Stone a fairly straight passage'.

Batten reverted to his normal powerhouse running in the second half and was soon putting Hull on the attack with a tremendous burst deep into enemy territory. The Airlie Birds continued to dominate with most of the play staying in Huddersfield's half of the field. Hull still could not add to their score, however, until Kennedy edged them into the lead with a superb penalty goal following the off-the-ball foul on Rogers.

Kennedy, who was having an outstanding game, then set up the match-clinching try when he slipped out a short pass to send Batten bounding for the posts. The goal was a formality for Kennedy and Hull never looked like being caught in the last ten minutes. At the final whistle Edgar Morgan, the former Wales Rugby Union international forward was chaired off the field to receive the trophy. It continued a remarkable run of progress by Morgan who two years earlier had made his Test debut after only seven Rugby League matches and was now the first Hull captain to lift the Yorkshire Cup only a few months after taking over the leadership.

Hull: E. Rogers; Stone, Collins, Batten, Kennedy; Whitty, Caswell; Beasty, Brennan, Bowman, Taylor, Morgan, Garrett.

Huddersfield: Oliver; Thorpe, McTigue, Wagstaff, J. Rogers; Edmondson, May; Schofield, Naylor, Clark, Fenwick, Gronow, Sherwood.

Hull v. Leeds

The Boulevard was the stage for some wonderful scenes during its 107-year history, but there was nothing quite like the occasion when it was packed with a ground record crowd of 28,798 for this memorable Cup-tie. The heaving mass spilled on to the pitch and delayed the kick-off until some sort of order was restored. But many hundreds remained congregated in the crescent area behind the posts and the players had a struggle to get on to the pitch. Some were actually lifted up by fans and carried forward.

Such scenes had never been seen at The Boulevard before and the first newspaper reports estimated the crowd at 35,000 on a day when over 100,000 attended the four third-round ties. It was not an all-ticket match, but the demand for seat tickets had been overwhelming and the Hull directors felt obliged to put a full page of explanations for their distribution in the match programme. The problem was simply that 8,000 had applied for the 600 three shillings seats. Leeds had suggested the seats should have been priced at five shillings and they could have sold the lot to their own fans.

So what was all the fuss about? Why did more people want to see this match more than any other played at The Boulevard before or since? Well, there was the long-standing traditional fierce rivalry between the two clubs, which exists to this day. Then there was the fact they were two of the biggest powers in the game at the time. A point to be confirmed at the end of the season as they held all the trophies open to them; Hull won the Championship and Yorkshire League title, while Leeds carried off the Rugby League Challenge Cup and the Yorkshire Cup. Indeed, had it not been for Leeds the Airlie Birds would probably have achieved the rare 'All Four Cups' feat as they lost to them in both the County and Rugby League Challenge Cup competitions.

Hull started slight favourites because of their remarkable record at Fortress Boulevard. They had lost only once in their last sixty-two home matches and that had been eighteen months earlier. The main danger to Hull was Eric Harris, the great Australian winger who was on a British record run of touching down in seventeen successive matches and it remained at that figure as the Airlie Birds gained some satisfaction in at least stopping him scoring in the Cup-tie.

Hull were at full strength apart from the absence of powerful prop Laurie Thacker and entered the field to a tremendous ovation. Although the match began in sunny, spring-like weather, the pitch was still heavy with mud from recent rain. There were also the remains of the frost-beating straw, which had been pushed back over the touchlines, and it would all churn up to make it a bog of a pitch.

The match was clearly going to be a forward battle between two uncompromising packs and the opening exchanges had the crowd baying for retribution at every doubtful tackle. It was blood-curdling stuff at times with first one team and then the other getting on top. Neither could break down the opposition and the first half ended 2-2 after Charlie Eaton's early penalty goal for Leeds, which went in off a post, had been cancelled out by Oliver's just before the interval.

Hull 4
  Goals: Oliver (2)

Leeds 5
  Try: F. Harris
  Goal: Eaton

Cecil 'Dicky' Fifield, Hull's Australian centre, whose touchdown was disallowed.

The second half was packed with unbearable tension as Hull did everything but score a try. Twice they were denied by referee Frank Fairhurst disallowing touchdowns. First Cecil 'Dicky' Fifield touched down after following up Miller's kick and the thunderous roar that greeted it turned to a groan when the referee ruled off side. Later the crowd's reaction was far more abusive when Oliver was also ruled off side after touching down. This latest disputed decision was a shattering blow for Hull as Leeds had just moved ahead with a wonderful try. When Fred Harris moved across to work the old scissors move with his winger, Hull followed Eric Harris inside only for the centre to retain possession and sweep round for a brilliant try.

It was now 5-2 to Leeds and a few minutes later the gap was down to one point after Oliver kicked his second penalty goal. The last quarter had the crowd in a constant state of hysteria as Hull piled on the pressure but just could not break the visitors' last-ditch resistance. Then came the double dismissal of Hull players that almost blew The Boulevard apart. Many did not see the incident but they howled like a lynch mob when, following the intervention of a touch judge, both George Barlow and Oliver were sent off.

Down to eleven men Hull's hopes of snatching victory looked hopeless. But they almost did it as Leeds started to panic. Twice they tried to kick themselves out of trouble only to give Hull chances of grabbing victory with drop goal attempts. Both were off target as were two penalty kicks by Miller, who had taken over the goal kicking from dismissed Oliver. The final whistle was the signal for a pitch invasion and a ring of police protection around the referee. Loud demonstrations went on for some time after the finish and heated debates about the match continued for years.

Hull: Miller; Gouldstone, Oliver, Fifield, Corner; Herbert, Courtney; Stead, G. Barlow, Carmichael, Dawson, Booth, Ellerington.

Leeds: Eaton; E. Harris, F. Harris, Parker, Brogden; Williams, Ralph; Dyer, Hall, Satterthwaite, Jubb, Casewell, Isaac.

Hull v. Widnes

9 May 1936   Championship final
Fartown, Huddersfield

This championship final became known as 'Joe Oliver's match'. Although all played their part in a magnificent team performance, it was Hull's captain who stood out with sixteen points from two tries and five goals. The international centre was a dominant force throughout, but particularly in the second half when he led the victory charge after the sides had been locked 2-2 at the interval. Oliver was such a great favourite with Hull fans that he probably inspired them to take up *Old Faithful* as the club's now famous anthem around this time. At thirty-three and after eight wonderful seasons at Hull, Oliver had become known as 'Old Faithful' (see Ern Shaw's cartoon opposite). So when Gene Autry made a hit record of the cowboy song in the mid-Thirties, Hull's fans latched on to it.

The turning point in the game came seven minutes into the second half when Oliver scored the first of his two tries. Jimmy Courtney set it up by moving quickly round to the open side of a scrum 20 yards from the Widnes line. The scrum-half was going well until the defence moved in and he shot the ball out to Cecil Fifield, who lobbed out a hurried high pass to Oliver. It was a difficult one to take and the Hull captain juggled with the ball before gaining control to sweep through for a well-taken try. Oliver tagged on the goal and a penalty after Freddie Miller landed a superb 45-yard drop goal. Then Oliver came up with a try that one report described as a 'masterpiece' and the *Hull Daily Mail* reported: 'Ten minutes from the end Wilson gathered a ball on the wing, cut inside and beat three men before giving a pass to Oliver who, instead of going for the far corner as it seemed he should have done, smashed straight ahead for the posts and hardly a man placed so much as a hand on him as he covered the 20 yards for a scorching try to which he added the goal.'

While the veteran Oliver dominated the game there were other outstanding performances, notably from young Miller. Although he was still under twenty-one, Miller had already played well over 100 matches for Hull and had an old head on his shoulders. The drop goal he landed was typical of many mighty efforts he scored in his long career. When Walter Bradley, the Widnes full-back, was harassed into making a hurried clearance kick Miller took it with ease 45 yards out and coolly sent the ball soaring nearly post high for a drop goal that stunned the opposition.

Despite a number of outstanding individual displays the *Hull Daily Mail* said it was still 'A triumph of a brilliant team, a combination of unquenchable enthusiasts imbued with a team spirit which cannot be surpassed by any other club in the league. To every member of the team honour is due for the wholehearted way in which they withstood the challenge of the determined Lancashire team and then made the issue safe with a great second half display.'

Hull, who had already won the Yorkshire League championship, had begun as favourites to lift the major title after finishing as leaders for only the second time under the old one league set up with sixty-one points from thirty-eight matches. They had beaten Wigan 13-2 in the play-off semi-final at The Boulevard, while third placed Widnes snatched a 10-9 win at Liverpool Stanley. The two finalists

Hull 21   **Widnes 2**
   Tries: Oliver (2), L. Barlow   *Goal:* Jacks
   Goals: Oliver (5)
   Drop goal: Miller

Brilliant cartoonist Ern Shaw's tribute to 'Old Faithful' Joe Oliver.

had not met during the season, but it was felt that Hull would have too much pace and power for their tenacious but limited opponents. Widnes were also weakened considerably by the absence of their two best players, clever scrum-half Tommy McCue and mighty prop Nat Silcock, who were both sea-bound for Australia with the Great Britain tour squad along with Hull loose forward Harold Ellerington. Even without Ellerington, Hull had a formidable pack that included the Barlow brothers, Charlie Booth and Laurie Thacker. All were to have a big say in Hull gaining midfield superiority. History supported the Airlie Birds, too, as Widnes were appearing in their first championship final, while Hull were aiming to make it three wins in as many finals although their last success had been fifteen years earlier.

Although Hull fans outnumbered their counterparts, the aggregate was disappointing with the attendance of 17,276 at Huddersfield's old Fartown ground the lowest at a championship final for several years. There was not a lot for either sets of supporters to cheer in a try-less first half, but there was plenty to admire in the ferocious tackling of both teams. Widnes, in particular, were forced to defend desperately as Hull piled on the pressure and had much more of the game territorially. They threatened to break clear on a number of occasions only to be

---

Hull: Miller; Wilson, Oliver, Fifield, Overton; Herbert, Courtney; Stead, G. Barlow, Thacker, L. Barlow, Booth, Dawson.

Widnes: Bradley; A.H. Evans, Topping, Jacks, Gallimore; Shannon, A. Evans; Higgins, Jones, Roberts, McDowell, Sherratt, Millington.

Winners of Rugby League Championship Cup and Yorkshire League Cup, 1935-36. *Back row*: Mr Drury, Mr Mennell, Mr Woods , Mr Broadwith, Mr Foster, Mr Chester, Mr Jackson. *Middle row*: Caswell (Trainer), C.Booth, L.Thacker, G. Barlow, S. Wilson, W. Stead, R. Corner, G. Bateman, L.Barlow, E. Overton, C. Fifield, Mr G. Miller (Chairman), J.Oliver (Capt), Mr H. Dannatt (Vice- Chairman), F. Miller, A. Carmichael. *Front row*: E. Herberts, J. Courtney.

held back by some extraordinary last-ditch tackling. 'Some of the tackling reached Test match standard in desperation' said a national newspaper report. 'Yet, in spite of it, Hull imparted into their attacks touches of the classical as befitted the champion side of the season. However, it was plain to see from an early stage that only a blunder on the part of the Hull defence could give Widnes much hope of success. While I cannot recall a single instance in which they ever looked like recording a try, the fortitude Widnes revealed in an heroic defence was the highest commendation.'

Widnes would be well satisfied to have withstood all Hull could throw at them to finish on level terms at the interval. The only scores had been penalty goals, one from Oliver after twenty-two minutes and an equaliser by Jacks ten minutes later. But the second half was an entirely different story. Hull set a hot pace from the start and with forwards and backs combining in impressive style it would not be long before Widnes finally cracked. The breakthrough came with Oliver's forty-seventh minute converted try. Miller followed up with his marvellous drop goal and Oliver slammed over another penalty goal after Jack Dawson had been obstructed by a desperate Widnes defender. It was now 11-2 to Hull and with hooker George Barlow giving the Airlie Birds plenty of possession from the scrums there was no stopping them despite Widnes continuing to perform heroics in defence. Hull's half-backs, Ernie Herbert and Courtney, were an impressive link between their forwards and threequarters to give Hull supremacy right across the field. Oliver's second converted touchdown came in the seventieth minute and just before the final whistle Laurie Barlow sneaked in for the final try. It only remained for Oliver to add his fifth goal and when the ball was returned to the field of play Fifield raced for it,

Sid Wilson, a strong-
running winger in the
championship final.

tucked it up inside his jersey and carried it off for a memento as the joyous Hull supporters invaded the pitch.

Oliver, of course, had a greater prize to collect and he received a tremendous reception when the championship trophy was handed to him by Sir Joseph Turner, the Huddersfield club's president. It crowned a wonderful season for the Hull captain, whose major scoring contribution lifted him to fourth place in the end of season try chart with thirty touchdowns and second in the points list with 244, only two behind Wigan's legendary Jim Sullivan. With form like this many felt that even though Oliver was at the veteran stage he was unlucky not to have joined Ellerington on Great Britain's Down Under tour. But Hull fans were happy enough as there was no doubt he was the major factor in bringing the championship trophy back to The Boulevard.

The Airlie Birds travelled home by train to a crowded Ferriby station where they were met by the Hull Lord Mayor and transferred to a coach that took them back to the city along Boothferry Road and Anlaby Road, with crowds cheering them all the way. A pile of congratulatory telegrams were awaiting the team including one from Hull City and another for Oliver from Mona Vivian, a music hall entertainer who had been appearing at the New Alexandra Theatre. Miss Vivian may have been a star, but the spotlight was now on Oliver and he became the toast of Hull.

HULL v. WIGAN

26 September 1936   League match
The Boulevard, Hull

Hundreds of dejected Hull fans missed one of the most amazing fight backs in the club's history when they streamed out of The Boulevard five minutes from the end of what had at that stage been a pathetic performance by the Airlie Birds. It was not just that Wigan were leading 12-3; it was because Hull had never looked like winning and had bumbled their way through the second half. The fans who made an early exit had had enough. Many must have been halfway home when they heard a mighty roar that shattered the gloom surrounding the ground, and another a couple of minutes later. What had happened? They were soon to find out as they were overtaken by thousands of joyous Hull fans who had stayed to the finish and were now hurrying home to tell of an incredible victory. The story they had to tell went like this:

After leading 4-0 at half-time, Wigan dominated the second half to be leading by nine points with only five minutes left and seemed to be just waiting for the final whistle. They looked certain to hold on to their record as the season's only unbeaten team after opening with four County Cup and League wins. Then Hull struck with a try that came out of nowhere; a score of pure silk compared with the shoddy fare that had gone before it. Scrum-half Jimmy Courtney started the weaving when he spun through a gap in the hitherto tight Wigan defence before putting in a kick. Harold Ellerington, showing rare pace for a loose forward in those days, won the chase to gather the ball in his stride as it bounced kindly for him. When he looked for support there was Hull's other half-back, Ernie Herbert, faithfully backing up alongside to take his pass and flash between the posts. Joe Oliver tagged on the simple goal to make it 8-12.

Hull fans would have probably settled for that with just over a minute left. At least they had finished on a high. But the players wanted more. When Wigan restarted with a kick down to Hull's right wing the home forwards surged back with a tremendous rolling attack that gathered momentum until it powered over the visitors' line where Laurie Barlow emerged from a mass of bodies as the scorer. Hull were now only a point behind with Oliver given the chance of snatching an incredible victory with the last kick of the match. The position could not be much more difficult, at an acute angle near the Threepenny stand touchline at the Gordon Street end. The tension was fit to snap. But Oliver was a veteran of Test matches and finals in which he had proved himself the man for the biggest of occasions. Now he took his time, waited until the crowd had hushed and then sent the ball soaring skywards. The gathering roar signalled a goal long before the touch judges' flags went up. Hull had pulled off the unbelievable. Less than five months after leading them to the Championship, Oliver was Hull's match-winning hero again and many recall that it was at the end of this memorable match that they first heard *Old Faithful* sung at the Boulevard. The Gene Autry cowboy song was popular at this time and it could have been taken up by Hull fans as an affectionate tribute to the veteran centre, known as 'Old Faithful'.

Ironically, for most of the match the Hull supporters had remained unusually quiet apart from the occasional shouts of witty derision from the Threepenny stand as the Airlie Birds made a succession of unforced errors. Some reports suggested

---

Hull 13
  Tries: Corner, Herbert, L. Barlow
  Goals: Oliver (2)

Wigan 12
  Tries: Morley, Seeling
  Goals: Sullivan (2)
  Drop Goal: Bennett

HULL FOOTBALL CLUB
(WINNERS OF THE YORKSHIRE LEAGUE CUP, 1935-36)

Caswell (*Trainer*), Overton, Booth, Stead, Dawson, Thacker, L. Barlow, Carmichael
G. Barlow, Wilson, Corner, Oliver (*Capt.*), Fifield, Miller
Ellerington (*inset*), Herberts, Courtney, Gouldstone (*inset*)

Ernie Herbert (*front row, left*), who scored Hull's first try in amazing fight-back.

Hull had not fully recovered from the tremendous fight they had put up to beat Leeds in a Yorkshire Cup-tie on the ground only two days earlier. In fact, the match against Wigan was Hull's fourth in nine days and they were clearly feeling the effects. Remember, the players were also working five or six days a week in those days. Whatever the reasons, there is no doubt Hull were well below their championship form for all but the last few glorious minutes of the match. One of Hull's few successes was young full-back Tommy Fletcher, who had made his first team debut only a week earlier and was now playing opposite arguably the greatest No.1 of all time – the legendary Jim Sullivan. Fletcher went on to make only twenty-eight appearances for Hull, but he could always look back on this as the day he matched the world's best. Reports praised him for his 'very courageous display'.

Despite their poor start Hull managed to restrict Wigan to a 4-0 interval lead, the only first half scores being a penalty goal from Sullivan followed by a George Bennett drop goal. But Wigan began the second half determined to put the game beyond doubt and it looked as if they had soon achieved it when brilliant passing produced an early try for Morley quickly followed by one from Charlie Seeling Jnr. Hull briefly halted the Wigan surge when Corner went in for a try before Sullivan added a simple penalty goal to give the visitors their 12-3 lead. With victory seemingly assured Wigan eased off and the action died down until Hull suddenly sparked into life with their amazing finish.

Hull: Fletcher; Overton, Oliver, Fifield, Corner; Herbert, Courtney; Stead, G. Barlow, Thacker, L. Barlow, Boddy, Ellerington.
Wigan: Sullivan; Morley, Innes, G. Davies, Ellaby; Bennett, H. Gee; Gregory, Golby, Edwards, Thomas, Sharrocks, Seeling.

Hull v. Hull Kingston Rovers

3 April 1953   League match
Boothferry Park, Hull

The first Rugby League match played at Boothferry Park was a huge financial success for Hull Kingston Rovers and a playing triumph for their great rivals. Hull City had generously loaned their soccer ground to hard-up Rovers free of charge and the result was easily their biggest ever 'home' crowd of 27,670, with the receipts of £3,280 a record for any rugby match in the city.

Excluding the Boothferry Park match, Rovers' average league attendance in 1952-53 was only 4,200 and Hull's 7,750. Thus there were obviously a huge number of City fans in the big crowd on that momentous sunny Good Friday afternoon. Rovers had been struggling to survive for many years and the continued loan of City's ground for their match against Hull proved to be a life saver over the next few seasons. It did little to halt their playing decline, however, and when they met Hull at Boothferry Park for the first time they were on the way to finishing twenty-eighth of thirty clubs. Hull were to end up in seventh place and started firm favourites to beat Rovers. But the form book could be discarded when these feuding neighbours met as Rovers had proved when beating Hull 16-9 at The Boulevard on the previous Christmas Day.

A little extra spice was added to the derby games then with the awarding of the Townend Trophy to the team who came out on top in aggregate over the season's two League matches. So Hull needed to win by seven points to retain the trophy donated in memory of Jack Townend, who had played for both clubs about fifty years earlier. Another link with the past came when a pre-match minute's silence was held for Laurie Osborne, a former Hull KR full-back who had died earlier in the week. With the solemnities over, a buzz of excited anticipation returned as the crowds continued to stream in right up to kick-off time. Boothferry Park was then a magnificent stadium and its packed stands and terraces provided a wonderful back drop to a great occasion.

It was certainly a fitting stage for Johnny Whiteley to produce the sort of performance that he was to repeat many times in a long career as one of Hull's greatest players. The twenty-two-year-old loose forward had not yet made his first Test appearance, but he was already being tipped as a Great Britain player of the future. Whiteley showed why with a brilliant display against Rovers, scoring two tries and having a big say in the other. He strode through the game in his unmistakable athletic style, drove the opposition back with long kicks to touch and smothered their attacks with superb cover tackling.

The Hull-born hero produced a classic piece of loose forward play to open the scoring when he picked up the ball from the base of an early scrum and shot away on a swerving run to put the ball down over the line scarcely before the Rovers pack knew what was happening. That was the only try in the first half and Whiteley opened the second half scoring when Carl Turner broke a tackle before sending the loose forward clear. Whiteley then turned creator as he combined with Colin Hutton to get little winger Gerry Cox scampering in at the corner.

The future star had clearly got the better of his loose forward duel with Alec Dockar, who had played for Great Britain six years earlier. He had also outshone a promising Rovers forward, Derek Turner, who played in the second row that day

---

Hull 13
Tries: Whiteley (2), Cox
Goals: Hutton (2)

Hull Kingston Rovers 2
Goal: Chalkley

Johnny Whiteley (right), who was outstanding in the first Rugby League match played at Boothferry Park, and rugged prop Bob Coverdale.

but was to become a keen rival for the Great Britain loose forward jersey when he moved to Oldham and later Wakefield Trinity.

The match was also a battle of wits and tactics between the two player-coaches, Hull centre Roy Francis and Rovers stand off Bryn Knowelden. Both were former Warrington and Great Britain players then in their veteran stage with Francis set to make much the bigger impact as a coach way ahead of his time and the man behind Hull's re-emergence as a real power in the Fifties.

There was another key duel at hooker where Sam Smith gave Rovers plenty of possession, but could not match Tommy Harris in the loose as Hull's Welsh international stood out with his trademark 'bomb burst' breaks. The Hull pack was beginning to combine as a force that was to dominate for almost a decade with props Mick Scott and Bob Coverdale giving Rovers a hefty sample of the future and second row Harry Markham punishing them with his hard, straight running.

Rovers did well to restrict Hull to only three tries, but they offered little in reply. Despite spending much of the first half in opposition territory they could not make a break through and trailed 5-0 at the interval, Colin Hutton having added the goal to Whiteley's try. Hutton also converted Whiteley's second try before Denis Chalkley scored Rovers' only points with a penalty goal.

Although the exchanges were always fierce, there was none of the savagery that marred some derby battles apart from a brief skirmish near the finish. In fact, one of the few casualties of the game was Widnes referee George Phillips, who broke a finger in a collision with Rovers forward Matt Anderson. Phillips, the top referee of his era, went off to have it strapped up but soon returned to resume his duties.

Hull: Watkinson; Watts, Francis, Hutton, Cox; Turner, Tripp; Scott, Harris, Coverdale, Hockley, Markham, J. Whiteley.

Hull K.R.: Chalkley; Tullock, McAvoy, Rushton, J. Moore; Knowelden, Daddy; Palframan, Smith, Tong, Turner, Anderson, Dockar.

HULL v. WORKINGTON TOWN

6 March 1954
The Boulevard

Rugby League Challenge Cup second round

A slow handclap earned this Cup-tie notoriety as it accompanied Workington Town's 'creeping barrage' that almost brought the game to a stand still. It also sounded the death knell of Hull's hopes of a first trip to Wembley for yet another year. A crowd of 20,000 had packed into The Boulevard expecting to see a rousing Cup-tie. What they saw was a game dragged down by the old play-the-ball rule that allowed a team to retain possession for as long as they could hold on to the ball. So while this game certainly does not come into the great or classic category, it was memorable in the sense that nobody who was there will ever forget it.

On a bog of a pitch made worse by tons of sand being trodden into heavy mud, Workington closed up the game shortly after Hull scored an equalising try in the forty-ninth minute. The visitors clearly decided to hang on for a draw with the better prospect of beating Hull after they had made the 180-mile midweek trek to Cumbria for the replay. With the scores locked at 5-5 Hull did everything they could to break down Workington's resistance, but when the opposition had the ball they were content to plough a slow furrow up the middle. Their forwards virtually fell at Hull's feet rather than risk losing the ball in the tackle or by passing. In one spell Workington kept possession for ten minutes before their 'creeping barrage' reached the halfway line. It was then that the slow handclap began, spasmodically at first and then taken up by Hull fans around the ground.

The Workington players were unmoved and kept to their unspectacular plan until referee George Phillips, probably as fed up as the Hull fans, penalised them for a play-the-ball offence. But Hull could not afford to play the same safety first game and lost the ball as they tried to open out play. Then it was back to Workington's endless succession of one-man drives. In the end the final whistle came as almost a relief to the frustrated Hull fans, who felt their team had not been so much robbed as paralysed by the opposition's tactics.

The farcical nature of the match increased the growing criticism of the play-the-ball rule, but nothing was done to break the monotony of one team retaining possession indefinitely until 1966 when the four-tackle rule was introduced, increasing six years later to six tackles. What was remarkable about the old rule is that it was not exploited more often. Workington's prolonged action – or inaction to be more precise – was exceptional. Even then, it seems incredible that there were thirty-three scrums in the game and Hull won twenty-three of them!

The pity of it all was that the match had been talked about and looked forward to ever since the second round draw paired the two together. They were as well matched as the 5-5 result suggested with Workington finishing fourth in the table and fifth-placed Hull only two points behind. Such was the demand to see the match that Hull introduced 'ringside' seating for the first time. This enabled spectators to sit all the way around the pitch within a few feet of the playing area and no barrier in between.

Hull went into the game full of confidence after stringing together an impressive run of eleven successive victories. They were also at full strength, while Workington

---

Hull 5
  Try: Conway
  Goal: Hutton

Workington Town 5
  Try: Dawson
  Goal: Risman

Bernard Conway, who scored Hull's only try.

were without both of their injured props John Henderson and Jimmy Hayton. At full-back for Workington was the remarkable Gus Risman, their captain who was just two weeks away from his forty-third birthday. Hull would again be relying on their mighty pack to dominate, while hoping the backs would snap up every opportunity in conditions that looked likely to force many errors. There was little sign of the dour stalemate early on as both teams showed enterprise and willingness to move the ball out despite the mud slowing down their best efforts. The conditions enabled both defences to stay on top and the first points came from a penalty goal by Hull's Colin Hutton after Workington infringed at a play-the-ball.

The tension intensified as Hull continued to do most of the attacking without being able to break down Town's stubborn defence. Then came a sudden turn of the tide and a shock for Hull fans when Workington broke away for a brilliant try. Johnny Mudge made the initial drive from inside his own half before handing on for Southward to race down the right wing. As full-back Hutton blocked his path the winger gave the ball back inside to Mudge, who sent Bob Dawson racing for the line. Although Risman failed with the goal kick he pushed Town further ahead with a twenty-fifth minute penalty for a scrum offence. That made it 2-5 and there was no more scoring before the interval.

Hull continued to do most of the attacking in the second half and finally got their reward in the forty-ninth minute after they increased the tempo with a terrific surge down the left that finished with Bernard Conway touching down too far out for Hutton to convert. Instead of the try sparking off an action-packed finish, it was the signal for Workington to shut up shop and the game ground to its inglorious end. There were far more thrills in the replay, which Workington won 17-14.

Hull: Hutton; Bowman, Riches, Turner, Watts; Conway, Tripp; Scott, Harris, Coverdale, Hockley, Markham, Whiteley.

Workington Town: Risman; Southward, Paskins, Gibson, Ivill; Archer, Dawson; B. Wilson, Lymer, Key, Mudge, Thompson, Ivison.

HULL v. HUDDERSFIELD

23 September 1954   Yorkshire Cup second round replay
The Boulevard, Hull

This was the most memorable match I ever saw, or at least it is the one remembered as the first really great game I had seen at the time. To check that I was not then just an easily impressed schoolboy, a look in the scrapbook was necessary, and there was the confirmation of what an outstanding match it was.

'It would be difficult to imagine a finer game of rugby football than was provided by Hull FC and Huddersfield last night' wrote Kingstonian of the *Hull Daily Mail*. 'Seldom have Hull played better football, and rarely has a match been seen on The Boulevard packed with so much excitement, thrills and skills. The score of 22-13 in their favour hardly represents the sum total of their superiority. Had Hull scored forty points they would not have been unduly flattered'.

The match was played only two days after Hull had earned the replay with a 7-7 draw at Huddersfield's famous old Fartown ground and the early Thursday evening kick-off meant many of the 16,038 crowd had come straight from work – or school. County Cup-ties were a big attraction then, but they added to the fixture congestion and the two midweek encounters came in the middle of a four matches in eight days spell for both clubs.

Although Huddersfield's glory days of the early post-war years were beginning to fade they still possessed a side that upheld the proud claret and gold tradition. Their great Australian winger Lionel Cooper was still there and his centre was an emerging young Mick Sullivan, who had not yet made the first of his record 46 Test and World Cup appearances for Great Britain. At the head of a solid pack was Dave Valentine, who was to lead Britain to victory in the first World Cup a few weeks later.

There were no established stars in Hull's team, but among a hard core of experienced veterans they had a number of young forwards who were starting to make a big impact. Unfortunately, Johnny Whiteley, the brightest of the prospects, was ruled out after injuring his shoulder in the drawn tie. Experienced centre Bill Riches retained his right-wing position after being switched there for the first tie to keep an eye on Cooper. He was to repeat his strong defensive display at The Boulevard after the Australian winger had early success with a try inside a minute.

A key man in the Hull side was Tommy Harris, who needed to win a good share of the scrums to keep the ball away from Huddersfield's dangerous backs and he responded by out-hooking Harry Bradshaw 21-11 in addition to making an impact in the loose with his short, sharp runs. The match was a triumph for Harry Markham, the big raw-boned second-row forward who repeatedly made deep inroads in the Huddersfield defence with his hard, straight running. He produced the individual highlight of the match with a great try after scattering four defenders on a devastating mid-field run to the posts.

Although the match was delayed for five minutes because of Huddersfield's late arrival it was the visitors who caught Hull napping with Cooper's try after only fifty seconds. Vintage Huddersfield play provided the opportunity as they kept the ball moving in great style to leave Hull's defence well beaten. Colin Hutton got Hull off

---

Hull 22

Tries: Riches, Markham, Conway, Watts
Goals: Hutton (5)

Huddersfield 13

Tries: Cooper, Rylance, Sullivan
Goals: Flint (2)

Harry Markham scored
a great solo try.

the mark with a penalty goal and they dominated the rest of the half with a succession of brilliant all-out attacks.

Huddersfield did well to hold them out until Arthur Bedford dashed past a gang of defenders to send Riches sprinting in for a magnificent try that received a tremendous ovation. The try gave a terrific boost to Hull's confidence and they began to produce the sort of rugby not seen at The Boulevard for a long time. It was mostly brilliant teamwork, but they went further ahead with Markham's marvellous solo try to which Hutton added the goal. Against the run of play Huddersfield hit back with a brilliant solo try of their own from Ron Rylance, who turned defence into attack as his pace took him sweeping through to the line. Rylance failed with the following goal kick but remained the biggest threat to Hull with his elusive running.

Hull's first half superiority was not reflected in their 10-6 interval lead and needed an early second half try to put them in total command. It came with a piece of brilliance to match Rylance's touchdown as Hull's stand off, Bernard Conway, zipped past a trio of Huddersfield players to go in near enough to the posts for Hutton to add the goal. Huddersfield's Sullivan then scored a try that gave an indication of what the future held for the youngster when he backed up a break by Cooper. There was some doubt about Cooper's pass that appeared to bounce forward and the crowd hurled their traditional abuse at experienced Widnes referee George Phillips. David Flint added the goal but that was soon matched by a penalty from Hutton to set up a grandstand finish by Hull.

They varied their play superbly and when Conway put in a kick to the left wing Ivor Watts took it on the bounce to scamper in at the corner. Hutton crowned the score with a soaring goal from the touchline. Victory was secure and Huddersfield's only reply was another Flint penalty goal.

Hull: Hutton; Riches, Turner, Francis, Watts; Conway, Tripp; Scott, Harris, Coverdale, Markham, Hockley, A. Bedford.

Huddersfield: Hunter; Henderson, Rose, Sullivan, Cooper; Rylance, Banks; Slevin, Bradshaw, Flint, Fairbank, Bowden, Valentine.

Hull v. Halifax

23 October 1954   Yorkshire Cup final
Headingley, Leeds

They threw it away. That was the view of many bitterly disappointed Hull supporters after seeing their team go down to yet another Cup final defeat. Post-match reports also suggested that Hull could have won this game if they had taken all their chances and not presented Halifax with too many, which they took.

Injuries also hit Hull hard, losing Keith Bowman midway through the second half and at one period being down to ten active players. Shortly after Bowman went off, Johnny Whiteley went to the touchline for treatment and Tommy Harris was left lying flat out on the field of play. But though referee Tom Watkinson looked anxiously at the prone figure, those were the days when the game could not be held up until the ball had gone dead. It seemed a long time before that happened and the Hull fans protested with a slow hand-clap after the hooker was finally treated and resumed playing. The loss of Bowman was a double blow as it meant Harry Markham, always a menacing runner in the second row, was taken out of the pack to fill the wing vacancy.

Under the heading 'Injuries put end to Hull's hopes', A.E. Birch of the *Rugby Leaguer* wrote: 'When this game comes to be talked about in the future it will be remembered as a game of thrills, a game of incidents, and yet another example of how Halifax – seemingly hard pressed for long periods – profited by some costly errors by Hull, and how their magnificent cover defence did the rest. But to both sides must go full marks for providing a pulsating, all-action game, right from the first minute to the last.'

This was the first of a series of big match clashes between the two teams in the Fifties, played with a ferocity that recalled the old beggars' saying of: 'From Hull, Hell and Halifax, Good Lord, deliver us.' If this match did not reach the bitterness of the Yorkshire Cup final replay a year later, it was tough enough and played with an intensity that kept the 25,949 absorbed throughout. Hull's young pack was still emerging as the force that would be such a power in the latter half of the decade and Halifax must take some of the credit for making them battle-hardened for what lay ahead.

But Hull's backs could not match those of Halifax, who included former New Zealand Rugby Union centre Tony Lynch, Test wingers Arthur Daniels and Dai Bevan, plus one of the greatest club pair of half-backs in Ken Dean and Stan Kielty. That was all in theory and on paper. In practice, Hull's unsung back division regularly got the better of star-studded opposition playing behind such a powerful pack. They also had the benefit of player-coach Roy Francis's vast experience in this match.

The best of Hull's backs on the day was probably Bernard Conway, a stand off with a neat sidestep and the pace to break clear. He also had good kicking skills as he showed when scoring Hull's first try, putting in a neat punt and winning the chase to touch down.

Halifax, who started as slight favourites, were penalised in the first few seconds and Colin Hutton immediately gave Hull's big following something to cheer with a well struck goal. Tysul Griffiths soon equalised with a penalty as both teams made a succession of errors in a tension-packed opening. Then came the first of Hull's

---

Hull 14
Tries: Markham, Conway
Goals: Hutton (4)

Halifax 22
Tries: Daniels (2), Ackerley, Pearce
Goals: Griffiths (5)

Keith Bowman (left) and Carl Turner, two of Hull's backs in the final.

costly errors. Hutton had two attempts at fielding a high kick, succeeding at the second go only to lose the ball in the tackle. Halifax pounced and a quick three-man strike ended with Alvin Ackerley grabbing a shock try to which Griffiths added the goal.

Another penalty from Hutton made it 7-4 to Halifax at the interval with Hull regretting having missed at least a couple of try chances. They regretted them even more not long into in the second half as Halifax forged further ahead thanks to some good old-fashioned scrum-half play by Kielty. His touch-finding kick to the corner brought a scrum heel from Ackerley and Kielty nipped round the blind side to send winger Daniels slicing through for the touchdown.

Griffiths tagged on the goal and it looked as if the game was slipping away from Hull until Conway's try revived their hopes. They rose a little more when Hutton hit a 30-yard penalty goal following two near misses and at 12-9 it was anybody's game again. Then came the injury to Bowman and Halifax took immediate advantage. After winning the ball against Hull's five-man pack, they whipped the ball out in brilliant style for Daniels to dash in for his second try. Griffiths added the goal and another when Les Pearce went in between the posts following a typical thrust by Lynch.

Trailing 22-9 and a man short, Hull refused to give up and raised their game for one last effort. It brought well-deserved reward when they worked the ball out to the left and makeshift winger Markham went over for a try goaled by Hutton. Hull's fans were now roaring them on as they sensed a dramatic late victory. But it was not to be as Hull were briefly cut down to 10 men and though they did well to hold back Halifax they could not add to their own score.

Hull: Hutton; Riches, Turner, Francis, Bowman; Conway, Tripp; Scott, Harris, Coverdale, Markham, Hockley, J. Whiteley.

Halifax: Griffiths; Daniels, Lynch, Todd, Bevan; Dean, Kielty; Thorley, Ackerley, Olsen, Pearce, Wilkinson, Callighan.

'For sustained suspense I have seen only one game to equal Saturday's Yorkshire Cup final; for the savage pace and spirit in which it was fought it stands alone. Here was rugby stripped of finesse and dignity. Here was a match which excited and repelled.' That was how the *Daily Mail*'s Derek Marshall described this ferocious battle and that's how I remember it.

Even as a fifteen-year-old youth in Headingley's South stand, I was both shocked and thrilled by it all. To say the match was a typical Cup-tie would be to call the First World War a skirmish. Yet it was also full of brilliant back play with Hull rallying magnificently from being 10-0 down to equalise with tries from wingers Ivor Watts and Keith Bowman.

Halifax did well to hang on as they finished the game with only eleven players after John Henderson was sent off in the fifty-seventh minute and Jack Wilkinson led off with a nasty facial wound in the closing minutes. Both departures followed incidents that gained the match notoriety. Henderson was given his marching orders for laying out Hull idol Johnny Whiteley and turning the exchanges from niggling and spiteful to all out brutality. The Halifax forward was pelted with objects from the main stand as he walked to the dressing room and the atmosphere became white hot. On the field the match finally erupted at a scrum from which Hull prop Bob Coverdale staggered out clutching his face. After treatment he went back and then Halifax prop Wilkinson reeled out of the re-formed scrum with a savage cut that needed four stitches.

Referee George Phillips was at a loss to know what had happened and to this day the versions vary. Even an emergency meeting called by the Yorkshire Rugby League to inquire into the incidents failed to come to a definite conclusion, while issuing a statement 'deploring' the incidents and instructing the management of both clubs that 'such practices must cease'. The statement brought a protest from Ernest Hardaker, Hull's chairman, who said it was completely uncalled for and tended to cause bad feelings between innocent players. 'I will certainly try to see that no harm is done to the players' reputations, whether they are Hull players or Halifax players,' he added.

Although the brutality of the exchanges surpassed all fears, it was always expected to be a fierce encounter between two sides that relied heavily on mighty, uncompromising packs. Hull were also out for revenge after being beaten by Halifax in the previous county final. They suffered a late blow when experienced full-back and goal kicker Colin Hutton was ruled out with an injury and young John Watkinson stepped in. But the youngster, the father of future Hull Kingston Rovers and Great Britain captain David Watkinson, gave a solid performance. He kicked two goals and went within inches of earning ever-lasting fame in the closing minutes when his 40-yard drop goal attempt almost snatched a dramatic victory only for it to soar wide.

Such a tight finish did not seem likely in a first half dominated by Halifax, who were 8-0 up after only thirteen minutes. Hull looked nervous early on and bad defensive

---

Hull 10   **Halifax 10**
  Tries: Bowman, Watts   *Tries:* Bevan, Henderson
  Goals: Watkinson (2)   *Goals:* Griffiths (2)

Ivor Watts (right) who had a try disallowed because of a forward pass. Tommy Harris (left) and Tommy Finn (centre) were also in Hull's Cup final line up.

errors enabled Halifax to exert immediate pressure that brought tries to Henderson and Dai Bevan. Tysul Griffiths converted the first try and when he added a penalty goal to make it 10-0, the odds against Hull winning lengthened considerably. But with their pack, led by captain Mick Scott, giving the opposition a pounding they gradually got back into the game and made a breakthrough just before half-time. Veteran centre Bill Riches unsettled Halifax's close marking by stabbing a grubber kick through their front line and Watts won the chase to touch down. That made it 10-3 to Halifax at the interval and set the stage for a bitterly-fought second half. Watts, for a forward pass, and Rowley Moat, unable to ground the ball, also had touchdowns disallowed as Halifax were put under increased pressure. At one stage it took them twenty successive play-the-balls to battle clear from their own line to halfway.

Although Halifax had the much better back line on paper, Hull had begun to show more enterprise as the first half came to a close with Bowman always taking a lot of stopping. Veteran centre Riches also needed careful watching and scrum-half Tommy Finn started to benefit from his forwards' dominance.

Following coach Roy Francis's interval pep talk the second half saw Hull's forwards take greater control, with Harry Markham, Bill Drake and Whiteley a terrific back three. Their superiority increased when Henderson was sent off and after two Watkinson penalty goals left them only three points behind, Hull took advantage of the extra man to get Bowman away down the right from near halfway. The winger cut between two defenders, broke through Griffiths' tackle and held off Bevan to plunge over the line for the equalising try ten minutes from time. Even as Bowman raced for the line two opponents were left trading blows 25 yards behind him. Watkinson was off target with his conversion attempt from near touch and the match continued to its bitter end with depleted Halifax much more relieved to hear the final whistle. But they were fit and ready for the midweek replay at Bradford's Odsal Stadium eleven days later when they held on to the Cup with a 7-0 victory.

Hull: Watkinson; Bowman, Turner, Riches, Watts; Moat, Finn; Scott, Harris, Coverdale, Markham, W. Drake, J. Whiteley.

Halifax: Griffiths; Daniels, Lynch, Palmer, Bevan; Dean, Kielty; Thorley, Ackerley, Wilkinson, Henderson, Schofield, Fearnley.

WARRINGTON v. HULL

21 April 1956   Championship semi-final
Wilderspool Stadium, Warrington

This was one of the greatest wins in Hull's long, proud history. It stunned the rest of the League. The result was unexpected enough, but the emphatic scoreline was almost unbelievable. Warrington were the League leaders and aiming to win the championship for a third successive season. They had not been beaten at home by a Yorkshire team for seventeen years and included legendary players such as Brian Bevan, Gerry Helme and Harry Bath.

In contrast, Hull had scraped into fourth place to appear in their first championship play-off for twenty years and most critics thought they lacked the all-round ability of their opponents. But the match was to prove the breakthrough for a side that went on to be a major force for the next four years. Under the guidance of Roy Francis – a coach years ahead of his time – they played to their strength and that was a mighty pack of forwards.

After the demolition of Warrington, Harry Sunderland, the former Australian tour manager turned journalist, wrote: 'The secret of Hull's success was the splendid all-round work of one of the best set of forwards in the League. I have rarely seen a better performance than that given by the last three men down, Harry Markham, Bill Drake and Johnny Whiteley.'

Markham may have lacked finesse, but his hard, straight running rocked Warrington time and again. Drake scored a vital late try, and Whiteley also had plenty of strength, but both ran like threequarters and made up for any lack of class Hull had in the backs. Up front, props Mick Scott and Bob Coverdale weakened the home defence with their constant battering, while hooker Tommy Harris's bombing runs were another constant threat. Hull's dominance belied the fact that Warrington's Tom McKinney won the scrums 26-18. Behind them, Hull's backs did their job in defence and even had the occasional surprise for Warrington on attack. Scrum-half Tommy Finn, in particular, made the most of his forwards' superiority as he gave them faithful support and was ready to feed off every break. He also linked well with his half-back partner Carl Turner and the pair moved smartly to send in Brian Cooper for the first try. Opposite Finn, former Test scrum-half Gerry Helme was expected to rule the midfield, but even his vast experience was of little use behind a beaten pack and Finn grew in confidence as Hull's forwards took over.

Even the great Bevan was rarely given a look in. At nearly thirty-two, Warrington's record-breaking Australian winger may have been past his incomparable best, but he had still finished the season with fifty-seven tries. Hull's two wingers that day had not totalled half as many between them. Keith Bowman had scored 23 and novice Brian Darlington managed 3 in three appearances. Bevan threatened occasionally with his dazzling side step and pace, but the Hull cover was always there to snuff him out.

Darlington, a top class amateur sprinter, had made his first team debut only a fortnight earlier and it was considered something of a gamble to pitch the lightly-built school teacher into such a big match. But he soon had the alarm bells ringing for Warrington when he kicked ahead and gave chase. Warrington survived that

---

Hull 17   **Warrington 0**
Tries: Cooper, W. Drake, Harris
Goals: Hutton (4)

Roy Francis, Hull's coach
and mastermind behind
their shock victory.

scare only to be forced into a succession of errors as Hull piled on the pressure in front of a 20,148 crowd.

Hull went close to scoring several times before Cooper went in for their opening try after twenty minutes. Hutton added the goal and already Hull fans were sensing they were witnessing a match to remember. Warrington tried to hit back, but even experienced Test stand-off Ray Price knocked on after Bath appeared to have put him through. They put Hull's line under tremendous siege without being able to add the finishing touch against some tenacious tackling and the vistors held out to take a well deserved 5-0 interval lead.

There was more of the same early in the second half and just when it seemed Hull, who were on £25 a man to win, might finally crack Markham scattered defenders in all directions on a thundering run to within feet of the home line. That was the turning point. Now it was Hull's turn to turn up the heat and Warrington started to wilt. A Hutton penalty goal on the hour edged Hull further ahead and in the last ten minutes they ground Warrington into the dust with two knock-out tries. Hull's forward were unstoppable at this stage and Scott sent Drake charging through a creaking defence for their second try and Harris blasted in for a third. With Hutton adding the goals to both tries, Hull supporters burst forth with a rousing rendition of their *Old Faithful* battle hymn.

The mobility of Hull's forwards had amazed many, but Francis had a simple explanation. 'I train my forwards like backs,' said Hull's coach. 'In fact, now and again in training, the backs pack down and the forwards line out.' Asked about the swift change of attacking direction that brought their two late tries, Francis said: 'Well, I don't believe in stringing out for an obvious cross-field passing movement. I tell my boys to line out in a sort of staggered formation so that when they receive the ball they can go either way.' Warrington did not know which way they went.

Hull: Hutton; Darlington, Cooper, Watkinson, Bowman; Turner, Finn; Scott, Harris, Coverdale, Markham, W. Drake, J. Whiteley.

Warrington: Fraser; Bevan, Naughton, Challinor, Horton; Price, Helme; Bath, McKinney, O'Toole, Ryan, White, Heathwood.

Hull v. Halifax

12 May 1956   Championship final
Maine Road, Manchester

The most memorable goal in Hull's history? It has to be the penalty Colin Hutton landed to win Hull the championship in the closing minutes of this tension-packed play-off final. Halifax were leading 9-8 with just two minutes left when Brian Darlington made a 30-yard break down the right. The amateur sprinter might have scored had he not been hampered by a leg injury sustained earlier in the game, but he still managed to make it to within a few yards of the Halifax line. Pressure on Halifax was now intense and they inevitably crept offside. Referee Charlie Appleton's whistle for offside pierced the crescendo of noise and immediately brought a sudden hush. The seconds were ticking away. What should Hull captain Mick Scott do? The great temptation was to take a quick tap and charge for the line that was so temptingly close. It seemed as if that is what he was going to do when he took the ball. Then Scott turned and beckoned for Hutton to go for goal. The full-back took the ball back to the 25-yard line and six yards in from touch. There were no tees to set up the ball then and Hutton had to make his own dent in the hard, almost grassless pitch. Then a few steps back, a pause and a little run up to send the ball soaring between the posts. Hull fans were still ecstatic a minute later when the final whistle heralded their first trophy success since they won the championship twenty years earlier.

The twenty-four-year-old Scott, who had only taken over as captain at the start of the season, explained his vital 'go for goal' decision later: 'I remembered Hutton's statement before half-time that he could do anything with the second half wind. I'd said I would let him have any shot within reasonable distance and I could not break my word.' Hutton summed it up as: 'The type of shot I'd been practising on Blackpool Borough's ground this morning. I knew it was a goal as soon as the ball left my boot.'

Halifax fans were desolate and with good reason to be, as they had seen their side pull back from being 8-0 down after fifty minutes and finish with three tries to two only to be foiled by a penalty in the seventy-eighth minute. But the *News Chronicle's* 'Hull deserved victory' headline summed up the general feeling. It was also a win against the odds as Halifax had started as slight favourites after finishing second to Hull's fourth. Despite the Airlie Birds having qualified for the final with a stunning 17-0 win at leaders Warrington, most neutrals reckoned Halifax's classier backs would swing the game their way after another mighty forward battle. The two packs had already clashed in several memorably torrid battles and there could be a few old scores to settle.

Hull coach Roy Francis was happy to let everybody, and particularly Halifax, believe his side would rely entirely on their formidable pack. He encouraged that belief by sending his forwards out to blast a way up the middle, but then they were to let the backs into the game. The plan worked as Hull's much maligned back division surprised the opposition with their enterprise and eager support play. Even the newly-formed half-back partnership of Carl Turner and Tommy Finn began to get the better of Halifax's inseparable Ken Dean and Stan Kielty.

Hull 10   **Halifax 9**
  Tries: Finn, Harris   *Tries:* Palmer, Daniels, Freeman
  Goals: Hutton 2

Tommy Finn is congratulated by Bill Drake after scoring Hull's second try. Mick Scott also joins in the celebrations.

But it was still Hull's pack power that brought the first try after a close-fought first half hour. Prop Bob Coverdale made the initial impact before slipping the ball out to loose forward Johnny Whiteley, who strode clear and then handed on for hooker Tommy Harris to finish the midfield drive between the posts. Hutton tagged on the goal to give Hull a 5-0 half-time lead. It was shortly after this that Darlington was injured in a tackle by Freeman and after struggling to stay on he left the field for a while. Even when the winger returned he was obviously far from fit and could hardly raise a gallop. But within ten minutes of the restart Hull had gone further ahead with a gift try. When Halifax tried to get Arthur Daniels away round the blind side of a scrum ten yards from their own line the winger tossed the ball back inside as Hull's quick-breaking back row cut him off. It was a panic move that was punished immediately by Hull scrum-half Finn, who nipped in to intercept and had touched down in the corner before the Halifax pack had broken up.

Although Hutton missed with his touchline goal attempt an eight-point lead had Hull fans singing *Old Faithful* as loud as they have ever done. They were soon silenced as Halifax powered back to take the lead with three tries in just over twenty minutes. It was their centres, New Zealander Tony Lynch and big Cumbrian Geoff Palmer who

Hull: Hutton; Darlington, Cooper, Watkinson, Bowman; Turner, Finn; Scott, Harris, Coverdale, W. Drake, Markham, J. Whiteley.
Halifax: Briers; Daniels, Lynch, Palmer, Freeman; Dean, Kielty; Thorley, Ackerley, Wilkinson, Henderson, Schofield, Traill.

HULL v. HALIFAX

Tommy Harris, who scored
the first of Hull's two tries.

did much of the damage. Palmer scored their first try with a powerful solo burst, cutting clean through Hull's hitherto tight defence. The try lifted Halifax's confidence and they started to get on top with Alvin Ackerley suddenly winning plenty of possession from the scrums. They moved the ball out in classic style and when Traill and Lynch sent Dean darting for the corner only a superb tackle by Hutton stopped the half-back from scoring. But a try was not long in coming and when Hull lost the ball near their own line, Lynch snapped it up to send Daniels dashing over in the corner.

Hull were looking tired at this stage with the injured Darlington a virtual passenger on the wing, but powerful charges by Scott and Markham gave them some relief as they took play deep into Halifax territory. Hutton then went near to edging Hull further ahead only to see his angled penalty shot go just wide of the posts. Still Hull maintained the pressure and when Harris carved out an opening for Drake the second rower had a chance to send Finn clear, but his pass went astray. Halifax took advantage of the let off to storm back, and another rampaging run by Palmer soon had Hull scattering back to defend and from the position gained Ken Traill sent Johnny Freeman over to put Halifax in the lead for the first time with only seven minutes left. Had young full-back Peter Briers converted any one of the tries Halifax would have gone on to be crowned champions, but he missed all three to leave their fans regretting the injury absence of experienced Tysul Griffiths, who had kicked a club record 147 goals that season. The last few minutes were agony for Hull fans as their team seemed to be on their last legs. Somehow they survived a succession of all out attacks before battering their way back. Scott led the way, setting a terrific example up front with a succession of battering charges. Then he shot out a pass to Darlington, who went through the pain barrier on a 30-yard run.

He went outside Freeman and inside Briers before being brought down six yards short of the Halifax line. Hull's fans sent up a deafening roar to urge their heroes on and they hardly heard the referee's whistle that signalled Halifax had been caught offside. Then they fell silent until Hutton landed his match-winning goal.

Although there was no official Man of the Match, Harris was a popular choice as the outstanding player. The Great Britain hooker was his usual dynamic self in the loose and also gave Hull a vital edge in the scrums opposite long-time rival Ackerley.

The *Sunday People's* Phil King echoed the views of other reporters in describing the match as 'One of the greatest championship finals ever. It had the spectators in a frenzy of excitement.' Another report said: 'There was everything the follower of the game could desire, fast open handling, spectacular pattern running and hard, tough forward play.'

It was Halifax's second successive final disappointment as only two weeks earlier they had lost to St Helens in the Rugby League Challenge Cup final at Wembley. It was sweet revenge for Hull, who had just suffered two successive Yorkshire Cup final defeats against Halifax. Apart from the glory, Hull's players were also rewarded with £33 pay packets.

There had been calls to switch the match to Headingley, Leeds, when two Yorkshire clubs won through to a peace-time final for the first time since 1938. But the RFL insisted on Maine Road remaining the venue and the attendance of 36,675 was the lowest of the eleven finals to be played at the Manchester City soccer ground. The game was also the first championship final to be televised, by regional station ABC, who paid £1,500 for the privilege.

Hull's championship-winning team line up before the final. *From left to right, back row*: Hutton, Coverdale, Whiteley, Bill Drake, Markham, Cooper, Watkinson, Bowman. *Front row*: Darlington, Turner, Scott, Finn, Harris.

HULL v. YORK

25 March 1957   League match
The Boulevard, Hull

Hull have had easier wins and have run up much higher scores, but this match stands out as a near-perfect exhibition of backs and forwards feeding off each other in devastating style. I have never forgotten it. However, I was a teenager then and recently wondered if time had added enchantment to the memory. A check with the *Hull Daily Mail* match report, however, confirmed that it was indeed an extra special performance by the reigning League champions.

'If any Hull supporter has seen more spectacular handling and backing up than that displayed by the Airlie Birds in Monday's game against York then I would like to hear from him,' wrote the Kingstonian. 'It must have been a long, long time ago! One old Hull supporter, who has been watching the Airlie Birds for over fifty years, told me he has never seen football to compare with it. Hull played beautiful, thrilling open football. York simply had no answer to this scintillating Hull, who played like real champions. The visitors were mesmerised.'

York were not a bad side in those days and finished eleventh in the 30-club table. But Hull were chasing a top four championship play-off place in defence of their title and only two days earlier had ended Leeds's club record run of 18 victories with a 27-4 hammering in another impressive performance at The Boulevard. Yet they started nervously against York before completely outclassing them. In fact, the visitors led 3-2 early on and Hull's nine tries were all scored in a dazzling last hour that had the 10,000 crowd in raptures. Hull's forwards and midfield backs ripped York apart so easily that only one of their tries went to a winger. The Airlie Birds led 17-3 at half-time and ran away with the game in the second half as they became more and more adventurous.

A probably unique feature of the match is that three brothers played in it, and each scored a try. They were Hull's famous Drake twins, Bill and Jim, plus younger brother Joe, who was a late inclusion because York's regular winger, Brian Smith, arrived late.

Tommy Finn led the try-scoring with a rare hat-trick in one of the most outstanding games of his 375-match career at Hull. The scrum-half was acknowledged as a craftsman, who worked closely with his mighty pack of forwards and put teamwork above any individual ambitions. But against York, the former St Helens half-back added that bit of extra flair to produce a superb all-round performance. He was here, there and everywhere, snapping up opportunities and creating play for others.

It was Finn who nipped in for Hull's first two tries to get them over their initial nervousness. Great support play enabled him to first finish off good work by Bill Drake and then take a reverse pass from Carl Turner, after the Welshman had made a superb break, to score a second. Finn completed his hat-trick early in the second half when nifty footwork took him past two bemused York defenders.

Turner, another long-serving Hull player, also produced a peak performance in the centre including a brilliant solo try after dummying and side-stepping his way to the posts. He also ran superbly in the middle of another spectacular move before

---

Hull 41
   Tries: Finn (3), Saville, Turner, Watts,
Scott, Jim Drake, W. Drake
   Goals: Hutton (7)

York 3
   Tries: Joe Drake

Colin Hutton, kicked seven goals
in an outstanding display.

sending Jim Drake charging over and late in the game he flashed through the middle before putting in a neat kick that Watts chased to touch down. Turner also won high praise for a strong defensive display. Co-centre Brian Saville breezed through the game in his usual graceful style, while Colin Hutton took every opportunity to link up from full-back in addition to kicking seven goals.

The foundations for the victory were inevitably laid by the Hull pack. They were often described as forwards who ran like backs, and never was that description more apt than against York, particularly when applied to their hooker and back row. Tommy Harris lived up to his 'Bomber' tag with a typically explosive performance, repeatedly blasting through the opposition in a manner that made him a hooker years ahead of his time. He still had the energy to win a majority of the scrums, which were then still fiercely competitive with much hard work done in the pack.

Rising above all in Hull's magnificent pack was Johnny Whiteley. Looking every bit the Prince of Loose Forwards, Whiteley strode through the game in majestic style. His long, athletic stride regularly put him in the clear and his classic distributive skills opened the way for his colleagues to break away. It was Whiteley's long pass that sparked off the bewildering move that led to Jim Drake's try and he was at the heart of another wonderful try. This time a typical break by Harris set up the position for Whiteley to swerve round three York players and send in Saville at the corner. The irrepressible Whiteley then paved the way for Bill Drake to touch down.

Second rowers Bill Drake and Cyril Sykes completed a free-running back-row trio, while props Mick Scott and Jim Drake added to the extraordinary mobility of the pack with their thundering runs. Scott finished off the try scoring when swift cross field passing gave him a big enough overlap to touch down with ease wide out. York's only try came early on when Joe Drake latched on to a big kick across field to score the game's first try and put the visitors into their surprise lead.

Hull: Hutton; Darlington, Saville, Turner, Watts; Moat, Finn; Scott, Harris, Jim Drake, Sykes, W. Drake, J. Whiteley.

York: Hunter; Joe Drake, Webster, G. Smith, Foster; Robinson, Riley; Moore, Long, Dickinson, Watts, Hansell, E. Dawson.

Hull v. Albi

15 April 1957
The Boulevard, Hull

European Championship

A superb last-minute drop goal by Mick Scott snatched Hull a dramatic draw over the French champions after a pulsating match. It left Hull needing only to beat Halifax to become the first European champions, which they did a week later. The competition seemed to have various titles, with Hull's match programme billing it as the International Club Championship, and it lasted for only that one season. Hull, as champions of the previous season, and beaten play-off finalists Halifax were the English qualifiers against French champions Albi and runners-up Carcassonne. The Airlie Birds took the title after topping the four-club table with five wins and a draw, their home and away English League matches against Halifax also doubling as European championship games.

Fitting extra matches into an already over-crowded fixture list was an even bigger problem then than it is now. The Monday night home game against Albi was Hull's fifth match in ten days as they were also going all out for a top four place in defence of the title. They had won the previous four, but seemed to be on their last legs when Scott came up with his match-saving drop goal, then worth two points. Albi looked certain to be 19-17 winners when the international prop blasted the ball 25-yards over a packed defence to give Hull the vital point.

Even without its dramatic finish, the match would have been remembered as a quality game of high excitement. The *Hull Daily Mail* reported: 'A draw was a fitting climax to this thriller, which kept 10,000 supporters roaring continuously and in a fever of excitement right to the last moment. Albi played grand football and really extended the Boulevarders, who, however, lacked some of their usual zip and speed, probably due to the fact that they have played five hectic games in ten days.'

France were quite a strong international force in the 1950s and Albi provided them with a number of top-class players. The home fans marvelled at the way Albi's players managed to keep the ball moving despite appearing to be well held, continually keeping Hull's defence at full stretch. They also excelled individually with winger Lapus scoring a wonderful solo try, beating several players on his weaving inside run to the posts. All this despite the pitch having been heavily watered following a dry spell, leaving pools and treacherous conditions underfoot.

Although Hull's support play was not up to its usual high standard they contributed plenty to the top class entertainment. Colin Hutton came in for most of the accolades after an outstanding game at full-back. In the middle of their hectic programme – this was their third match in four days – Hull made a few changes from their regular line-up, including Alan Holdstock standing in for Test hooker Tommy Harris and winning a majority of the scrums. An early scrum infringement enabled Andre Rives to put the Frenchmen in front with a penalty goal and the tit-for-tat pattern of play was soon established as Hutton replied with one for Hull. Both sides started throwing the ball out in great style and after there had been narrow misses at both ends Hull went ahead with a gem of a try created by Geoff Dannatt, who dodged past three defenders before sending in Tommy Finn.

Hull 19
Tries: Moat, Finn, Cole
Goals: Hutton (4)
Drop goal: Scott

Albi 19
Tries: Lapus, Fabre, Courviegnes
Goals: Rives (5)

The centre spread of the programme for Hull's home match against Albi.

The lead was short lived as Lapus swept in for his great try and Rives added the goal to put Albi ahead. They maintained the pressure and a powerful break by Jean Marie Bes gained the position from where Bernard Fabre went over near the posts. Rives tagged on the goal and at 5-12 Hull fans must have feared the worst. But they got behind their team and Keith Bowman had them in full voice as he crashed through three tacklers on a thundering touchline run before being overwhelmed just short of the corner flag. Hull maintained the momentum and flashed the ball across the field for lanky second rower Colin Cole to justify his first team call with a smart dummy that took him over in the corner.

An 8-12 interval scoreline promised a rousing second half and the fans were not to be disappointed. Within minutes of the restart they were applauding a marvellous try by Rowley Moat plus a conversion from Hutton that edged the home side in front. Johnny Whiteley set it up with a typical break, beating a trio of Frenchmen before sending Moat haring for the line. As the tempo increased Albi became even more adventurous and regained the lead with a rather fortunate try by Courviegnes, who snapped up a loose ball before sneaking over. A simple goal from Rives made it 17-13 to the Frenchmen. Hull fans thought Courviegnes was offside when he picked up the ball and let Wakefield referee Ron Gelder know in their usual colourful way. But they were much quieter when he ignored French protests and awarded Hull two quick penalties, which Hutton turned into four points to level the scores.

In a tension-packed finish both sides continued to give away penalties and Hutton missed a chance to edged Hull ahead with another goal shot. It looked like being an even more costly miss when Rives kicked a penalty from near halfway to put Albi 19-17 in front. Then Scott came to the rescue with his equalising drop goal.

Hull: Hutton; Bowman, Dannatt, Turner, Coulman; Moat, Finn; Scott, Holdstock, J. Drake, W. Drake, Cole, J. Whiteley.
Albi: Rives; Lapus, Corduries, Courviegnes, Aymes; Fages, Fabre; Bes, Combettes, Roques, Verdie, Berthomieu, Blanc.

HULL v. BARROW

Controversy surrounded this match, with many Hull supporters protesting at the club's decision to forfeit ground advantage and switch it to Hull City's Boothferry Park soccer ground. The move was necessary because Hull's Boulevard pitch had been dug over for re-seeding. Hull Kingston Rovers had already played a few of their home matches against Hull at Boothferry Park, but this was the first time the Airlie Birds had a hired the ground and it was a far from popular move. There were also objections to the kick-off time of 3 p.m., which clashed with the televised FA Cup final and this was sited as the main reason for a 'disappointing' crowd of 19,980.

Hull went into the match as defending champions and favourites, having finished second to Barrow's third. They were also totally focussed on the game as opposed to their opponents who were due at Wembley for the Rugby League Challenge Cup final a week later. Whatever their state of mind, Barrow certainly went into the match with the best of intentions and fielded their strongest line-up. Barrow were also the last team to beat Hull before they began a ten-match unbeaten run and had a team full of stars, including their greatest player of all time in Willie Horne at stand off. Despite their wealth of outstanding players, Barrow were ripped apart by Hull's mighty pack well supported by an eager back division. Although speculation continued after the match about how much Barrow were pre-occupied with their forthcoming Wembley appearance, several reports dismissed it as significant.

'Excuses for Barrow are so much poppycock,' said one national newspaper report. 'This was an utter rout of a Barrow team outpaced, out-generaled and beaten in every section of the game. No team living would have survived against this remarkable display of passing in which the entire Hull team repeatedly took part. Forwards and backs alike handled with great skill.'

Although Barrow put up some early resistance and did not concede a try until the sixteenth minute they began to wilt in the bright sunshine and were caught in a stampede as Hull kicked up the dust and raced in for eleven touchdowns. They were 16-0 up at half-time and had 26 points on the board before Barrow scored their first try in the forty-ninth minute. The Wembley finalists had good reason to give up when they were reduced to twelve players for the last twenty minutes following the departure of injured Goodwin, but despite being 32-3 down they came back with three tries to make the scoreline a little more respectable. In fact, it was Hull who appeared to ease up once a place in the Championship was assured.

Overall, though, Barrow had no answer to Hull's power play. With Tommy Harris winning the scrums 17-12 and their pack totally dominant in the loose the Airlie Birds' backs were able to outshine the likes of Horne and company. All of Hull's threequarters plus scrum-half Tommy Finn scored tries as they combined superbly with the forwards. Finn's try was probably the best solo effort of the game as he zipped past four defenders in a dazzling 25-yard run to the posts. The right flank combination of winger Stan Cowan and centre Geoff Dannatt was a revelation, each scoring two tries. The entire Hull pack received plenty of plaudits

---

Hull 45
  Tries: Cowan (2), Dannatt (2)
     W. Drake (2), Finn, Watts, J. Drake,
     Sykes, Turner
  Goals: Hutton (6)

Barrow 14
  Tries: Rea (2), Barton, Ball
  Goal: Ball

The programme

RUGBY LEAGUE
CHAMPIONSHIP
SEMI-FINAL

★

HULL
VERSUS
BARROW

at BOOTHFERRY PARK, HULL
by kind permission of HULL CITY A.F.C.

Souvenir
Programme 3d.

Nº 5661

with the Drake twins coming in for special mention. Second-rower Bill went over for two tries in classic style, while the more rugged Jim belied his typical prop forward image by sidestepping over for another.

Although Hull dominated the early stages, they had only a Colin Hutton penalty goal to show for their efforts until Finn's solo try broke Barrow's resistance. Hull began to open up and it was not long before the ball was flashed along the line for Cowan to go in for his first try. A few minutes later Ivor Watts was scampering in on the other wing. Although Barrow were contributing plenty to a fast, open game they lacked Hull's finishing touch and went further behind when more brilliant passing ended with Dannatt racing over.

That gave Hull their 16-point interval and any hopes of Barrow getting back into the game were soon dispelled when Bill Drake finished off another spectacular move by kicking ahead and touching down. Brother Jim then came up with his try and with Hutton adding goals to both touchdowns Hull were out of sight. They continued to keep the ball alive at every opportunity and Finn overdid it a little for Barrow's Johnny Rea to flash in with an interception near halfway and race clear for the visitors' first try. Normal service was soon resumed, however, with Dannatt and Cowan adding further tries for Hull following more bewildering passing moves that had the crowd constantly cheering.

It was now 32-3 and when Hull started to ease up Barrow took advantage for Barton and Rea to score tries and Ball add a goal. The Barrow reply stung the Airlie Birds back into action with tries quickly flowing to Carl Turner, Bill Drake and Cyril Sykes before Ball scored a late consolation try.

A sad note to end on is that Harold Bowman, one of Hull's greatest forwards in the 1920s, collapsed and died at the match. He was the father of Keith Bowman, a winger for Hull who was in the dressing room at the time, but was not down to play against Barrow.

Hull: Hutton; Cowan, Dannatt, Turner, Watts; Moat, Finn; Scott, Harris, J. Drake, Sykes, W. Drake, J. Whiteley.

Barrow: Ball; Lewthwaite, Jackson, Rea, Castle; Horne, Harris; Woosey, Redhead, Barton, Grundy, Goodwin, D. Wilson.

HULL v. OLDHAM

18 May 1957   Championship final
Odsal Stadium, Bradford

What a difference a year makes. Just twelve months after being hailed as Hull's hero for kicking a late penalty goal that won them the championship, Colin Hutton experienced the agony of fluffing a much simpler attempt that would have retained the trophy in similar dramatic fashion. Hull were trailing 15-11 with only three minutes left when against the run of play Stan Cowan snapped up a loose Oldham pass and raced 40 yards to the line. He placed the ball down about 12 yards to the right of the posts and the goal kick should have given no trouble to Hutton, who had already kicked a then Hull record 166 that season. The crowd of 62,199, that had been at fever pitch of excitement for most of the game, was now hushed as Hutton made his preparations. About thirty seconds later came the thud of his boot and then an amalgam of Hull groans and Oldham cheers as the ball soared high – and wide.

The dramatic finish was a fitting climax to what the *Daily Sketch* described as 'the most exciting Rugby League tournament final ever'. Perhaps, it was not quite that, but it was packed with incidents and controversy. Hull were leading leading 11-5 when the match turned on a crucial decision in the fiftieth minute as referee Matt Coates penalised Hull forward Cyril Sykes for not playing the ball quickly enough. But Sykes had been stunned in a crash tackle and was still dazed as he rose unsteadily to his feet. Despite Sykes having to go off for treatment the referee stood by his decision and Oldham's Bernard Ganley banged over the goal from near halfway. 'I was hurt in the tackle and my knee reflexes seemed to be paralysed,' said Sykes later and the referee admitted: 'I did not realise at the time that Sykes was injured.'

From being six points down, Oldham were now only a try and goal from taking the lead and they managed that just eight minutes later when Dennis Ayres went between the posts and Ganley added a simple goal. In the final analysis it will be seen that Ganley's controversial penalty goal and Hutton's late miss cost Hull the game, but it would be unfair to blame the Airlie Birds' full-back for the defeat. He had a fine game generally and, ironically, it was his goal kicking that earned Hull a 6-5 interval lead with two superb penalties and a calmly taken drop goal just before half-time. Johnny Whiteley played a fine captain's role and Tommy Harris won the scrums 18-13.

Although Hull were a little unlucky to lose, the general neutral view was that Oldham just about deserved victory and their reported £40 per player wage after scoring three tries to two and having finished six points clear of their second-placed opponents. Jack Bentley of the *Daily Express* summed it up thus: 'Hard luck on Hull again… but justice was done. Oldham were the class side, the footballing side. Sometimes they over-elaborated, but the dash and glitter of their backs, particularly centre Alan Davies and winger John Etty were a constant menace to the first class Hull cover. But a big bouquet to Hull. Great champs they were, great losers they are.'

Although Oldham started as favourites, Hull went into the match full of confidence after an unbeaten run of eleven matches, including the impressive 45-

---

Hull 14
Tries: Cowan, Turner
Goals: Hutton (3)
Drop goal: Hutton

Oldham 15
Tries: Etty (2), Ayres
Goals: Ganley (3)

Stan Cowan, who scored Hull's late try.

14 semi-final defeat of Barrow. Hutton gave Hull the lead after two minutes with a penalty goal from near touch and they continued to have territorial advantage although Oldham always looked capable of striking from any part of the field. They emphasised that against the run of play when they whipped the ball out wide for Etty to brush aside two defenders on a powerful burst to the line. Ganley's goal made it 5-2 to Oldham before they fell behind to Hutton's penalty and drop goal.

Hull surged further ahead early in the second half with a marvellous try. Harris flung a long pass out to Whiteley and the loose forward strode swept past three opponents in majestic style. With the cover closing in, Whiteley switched the ball back inside for Carl Turner to touch down between the posts. Hutton's goal was a formality. Hull were well on top at this stage and looked to be heading for victory until Ganley's debatable penalty goal following the injury to Sykes got Oldham back into the game. The League leaders took full advantage to increase the tempo and Davies carved out an excellent try for Dennis Ayres. Ganley's goal put Oldham a point ahead and they seemed to have clinched victory when a Hull attack went horribly wrong. Stan Cowan was the culprit as his kick ahead went straight into the hands of Oldham's Pitchford, who turned defence into devastating attack. The scrum-half streaked away before handing over for Etty to finish off in the corner.

A few dejected Hull fans started to trickle away to the exits until they were stopped dead in their tracks by a sudden roar. When they turned round there was Cowan making up for his error by pouncing on an Oldham mistake and racing away for the try that gave Hull a great chance of snatching victory. But it was not to be as they suffered their first defeat in a championship final after four successes.

Hull: Hutton; Cowan, Dannatt, Turner, Watts; Moat, Finn; Scott, Harris, J. Drake, Sykes, W. Drake, J. Whiteley.

Oldham: Ganley; Cracknell, Davies, Ayres, Etty; Daley, Pitchford; Jackson, Keith, Vines, Winslade, Little, Turner.

HULL v. OLDHAM

3 May 1958   Championship semi-final
Watersheddings, Oldham

Thrashed 43-9 at Oldham only two weeks earlier, Hull were given little chance on their return trip. But the Airlie Birds rose to the task magnificently to pull off one of their most memorable victories despite being down to twelve men for the last seventeen minutes following Tommy Harris's dismissal. Oldham had finished as League leaders for a second successive season after winning their last eleven matches and were expected to retain the championship they had won by beating Hull in the final a year earlier. But this was the sort of challenge fourth-placed Hull relished. Coach Roy Francis had given nothing away when Hull succumbed to Oldham in their last League match of the season, yet he selected the same team apart from Geoff Dannatt replacing Gordon Harrison on the left wing.

They were still without injured Jim Drake, but Brian Hambling was to prove a worthy understudy. Hambling also did a fair job when taking over as hooker following Harris's sending off. Harris was sent off for a perfect right cross that flattened Great Britain tour colleague Frank Pitchford after the Oldham player had been involved in an incident that left Hambling injured on the ground. The hooker knew it was a bad foul and he was on his way to the dressing room before referee Matt Coates could order him off. Hull were leading 20-3 at the time and their twelve men did well to hold out Oldham until Dennis Ayres scored a consolation try for the home side and Ganley added the goal.

Several other players were fortunate not to have been sent off earlier in a ferociously fought game. Derek Turner, Oldham's fiery loose forward, was twice spoken to and had his name taken by the referee. Others were also lectured, but there was still plenty of spectacular play with Hull kicking up the dust on the bone dry pitch as they matched Oldham's all-out attacking rugby.

Allan Cave of the *Daily Herald* admitted he had given Hull no chance of winning and then wrote glowingly: 'Hull gave a power show that had to be seen to be believed. Oldham, the side I thought had everything, had nothing left at half-time, when it was 18-3. Hull's forwards ran Oldham into the ground. I have never seen anything like the football Hull produced. No wonder Oldham couldn't live with it.'

Johnny Whiteley was an inspiring leader for Hull and completely outplayed Turner, his keenest rival for the Great Britain loose forward jersey. While Turner's uncompromising style trod the border line of legality and sometimes stepped over it, Whiteley relied on his brilliant skills to dominate the mid field. Bill Drake also moved like a threequarter in the second row, while Mick Scott provided the power up front with a series of hefty charges that rocked Oldham time and again. With Harris producing his trademark bomb-burst runs, Hull's forward supremacy allowed their workmanlike backs to outshine Oldham's star-studded back division.

There was controversy in the build up to the game with Hull fans protesting strongly against a 6 p.m. kick-off after Oldham switched it from the Saturday afternoon to avoid a clash with the televised FA Cup final. Despite their objections, Hull fans again travelled in their thousands to boost the attendance to a ground capacity 23,000.

Hull 20   **Oldham 8**
  Tries: Watts, Cooper, W. Drake, Sykes   *Tries:* Dufty, Ayres
  Goals: Bateson (4)   *Goal:* Ganley

Cyril Sykes, blasted through for Hull's last try.

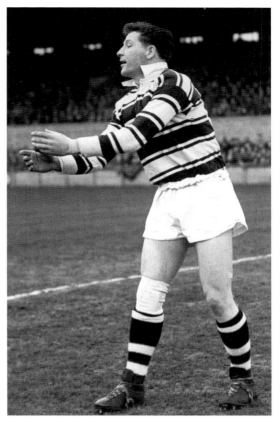

Hull soon displayed their intent as their pack charged at and dumped the opposition with a ferocity that gained them immediate dominance. Within three minutes they had taken the lead. Hambling instigated the score with a terrific break before sending Tommy Finn scampering over to the right where he sent Ivor Watts in at the corner. Oldham took almost a quarter of an hour to get into Hull's half and then, much against the run of play, they opened their account when Roger Dufty went over near the corner flag to make it 3-3. It was a false dawn for Oldham as Hull powered back and completely demolished them with a devastating three-try reply before the interval.

Bateson edged Hull in front with a penalty goal and added the conversion when Brian Cooper scored their second try after Cyril Sykes opened the way with a decisive break. The next try sent Hull fans wild as Oldham were turned inside out by a bewildering move. Cooper began it near the touchline when he picked up the ball from a short kick and back passed to Watts, who cut inside on a weaving run. He then linked up with Bill Drake, who strode away for a glorious try. Drake was prominent again when he and Whiteley tore another big hole in the home defence and Sykes backed them up to blast his way through Ganley's tackle and go over near the posts. Bateson tagged on the goal to give Hull their remarkable 18-3 interval lead.

The second half failed to bring the thrills of the first forty minutes as tempers became frayed and Hull's only second half score was a goal by Bateson after Oldham prop Ken Jackson was penalised for punching. After handing out a number of warnings the referee had no option but to dismiss Harris. Even against only twelve men, Oldham struggled to find a way through until Alan Kellett sent Ayres away for a try goaled by Ganley. But there was no chance of an Oldham victory and Hull fans were giving full voice to their *Old Faithful* hymn long before the finish.

Hull: Bateson; Watts, Cooper, Saville, Dannatt; Broadhurst, Finn; Scott, Harris, Hambling, Sykes, W. Drake, J. Whiteley.

Oldham: Ganley; Cracknell, Ayres, Davies, Etty; Kellett, Pitchford; Jackson, Keith, Dufty, Winslade, Little, Turner.

HULL v. WORKINGTON TOWN

17 May 1958   Championship final
Odsal Stadium, Bradford

Champions again! Hull won the top four play-off for the second time in three seasons and did it once more as outsiders from fourth place. But this time they triumphed comparatively comfortably with none of the drama of their 1956 victory over Halifax or defeat by Oldham a year later. Both those matches were decided by a goal kick in the dying minutes, while the defeat of Town looked certain long before the finish.

Like Halifax two years earlier, Workington went into the championship final a week after the depression of defeat at Wembley. They also suffered a major blow against Hull when reduced to twelve men after only twenty-five minutes when their outstanding second row forward Cec Thompson was carried off on a stretcher with an ankle injury.

However, there was no doubting Hull deserved the victory after overcoming their own setbacks of being able to field only half of their regular mighty pack. As Jack Bentley of the *Daily Express* wrote: 'Even if Workington hadn't lost Cec Thompson I'm convinced Hull would still have won. Hull had the power and drive, the pace and the ideas. Workington were beginning to show signs of the exhaustive strains and exertions of the last few months even as Thompson came a cropper. They had more of the ball than Hull, sometimes keeping possession for minutes on end, but they could not find a way through.'

Hull's victory was a tribute to their reserve forward power. The absence of such outstanding forwards as the Drake twins and Tommy Harris seemed to halve their fire power and swing the balance towards Workington. But the Airlie Birds' trio of reserves rose to the occasion magnificently in a now completely Hull-born pack. Brian Hambling, who had already proved his worth with a terrific game against Oldham in the semi-final as a replacement for injured Jim Drake, came up with a repeat performance in the front row. Young A team hooker Alan Holdstock was far from overawed at standing in for the world's top No.9 Tommy Harris, who had been suspended for two matches following his semi-final dismissal, working hard in the loose and winning a fair share of the scrums. Peter Whiteley soon had the Hull fans cheering him on after they had greeted with groans the late programme change announcement that he had replaced injured Bill Drake. Peter Whiteley never came near to emulating the feats of his brother, the great Johnny Whiteley, during his career but on this occasion there was little to choose between the pair. Johnny led Hull in majestic style, while Peter provided faithful support in one of his best ever games.

As ever, Hull owed much to the experience and example of Mick Scott up front. Many thought Scott was unlucky not to be named for that year's Great Britain tour squad and he gave the selectors an embarrassing afternoon with a display of power and panache. After battering the Town defences with a succession of mighty charges, Scott showed remarkably agility for a big man by swerving nimbly round stand off Harry Archer to score a second-half try. The big prop had earlier shown his distributive skills by throwing out a long pass that put Brian Cooper through for a try. Work horse second rower Cyril Sykes produced his usual non-stop efforts in

---

Hull 20
Tries: Cooper, Finn, Scott, J. Whiteley
Goals: Bateson (4)

Workington Town 3
Try: Southward

Hull's Brian Cooper moves in to tackle Jock McAvoy.

attack and defence to complete Hull's pack supremacy. Behind them their much under-rated backs also had the edge on Workington's with Cooper in particular having an impressive game in the centre.

Both clubs provided tourists for the Great Britain trip to Australia and New Zealand with the main party already having left for Down Under. Flying out to join them after the final would be Hull's Johnny Whiteley and Harris plus Archer, Brian Edgar, Ike Southward and Bill Wookey. Wookey was one of two of Workington's Wembley line up who missed the championship final because of injury, the other being Andy Key. Ken Faulkner came in on the wing for Wookey and Tom Stamper replaced Key at prop. The loss of Key was a blow for Town. But they still had a typically strong Cumbrian pack, led by Edgar, one of the greatest forwards of the era who was to give Hull plenty of trouble.

Workington went ahead soon after Thompson was carried off. A thundering run by Edgar and a pass out to Southward saw the winger dash in at the corner. It was a rare breakaway by Workington whose earlier play had consisted mainly of short midfield forward rushes and Hull's more adventurous style soon brought them their reward with Cooper's try, superbly goaled by Peter Bateson. Workington did well to hold Hull to a 5-3 interval lead before crumbling away in the second half. Another long run by the impressive Cooper gained the position from which Johnny Whiteley punched through from a play-the-ball for a try to which Bateson added a simple goal. There was no stopping Hull at this stage and the two Whiteleys combined to send Scott over for his try with Bateson tagging on the goal. Johnny Whiteley was there again to set up another try a few minutes later, moving swiftly to get Tommy Finn romping in round the posts for Bateson to complete his 100 per cent kicking success with a fourth goal. Victory was assured and *Old Faithful* echoed once again on the terraces.

Hull: Bateson; Watts, Cooper, Saville, Dannatt; Broadhurst, Finn; Scott, Holdstock, Hambling, Sykes, P. Whiteley, J. Whiteley.

Workington T: McAvoy; Southward, O'Neill, Leatherbarrow, Faulder; Archer, Roper; Herbert, Eden, Stamper, Edgar, Thompson, Eve.

HULL v. FEATHERSTONE ROVERS

11 April 1959   Rugby League Challenge Cup semi-final
Odsal Stadium, Bradford

Hull are on their way to Wembley! After many frustrating failures, the Airlie Birds were finally winging their way to the twin towers, thanks to a brilliant hat-trick of tries by twenty-year-old George Matthews – and that pack, of course. Three successive championship finals, including two victories, in the immediate previous seasons had given Hull fans plenty to cheer about, but a trip to Wembley is what they dreamed about. Now they were going and their hero was young Matthews. It was only a year earlier that the former England amateur international from Barrow had made a memorable professional debut for Hull reserves.

He had since made steady progress but it was not until the semi-final against Featherstone Rovers that the Rugby League world generally took notice of the talented stand off. Then he hit the headlines by scoring all three of Hull's tries. Ironically, it was at half-back that Featherstone were expected to have their one big advantage after Joe Mullaney had given an inspiring performance in their shock third round defeat of League leaders St Helens. Mullaney was regarded as one of the best stand offs of the time with lots of experience and ability. What he did not have was a pack quite as powerful as Hull's. That is why Matthews was given almost the freedom of the field as Tommy Harris won the surprisingly few scrums 10-6 and the Hull forwards took command in the loose.

Hull went into the match still as reigning champions, but they had virtually given up hope of reaching the top four play-offs for a fourth successive season. They were lying sixth in the table, with Featherstone seven places below, and were putting all their energy into reaching the Rugby League Challenge Cup final for the first time since 1923. Hopes were high among their fans in the crowd of 52,131, who packed into Odsal on a wet and miserable afternoon. The match turned out to be a triumph for coach Roy Francis's tactical planning, which he had outlined to the press before the game. His plan was simply to win plenty of possession, blot out any threat from the Featherstone half-backs at source and let Hull's forwards do the rest. He had told Matthews and his scrum-half partner Frank Broadhurst to follow the Rovers pair everywhere – 'even if they left the field'.

Following Hull's roaming pack of forwards came naturally to Matthews and it brought him early reward as he took Johnny Whiteley's pass to glide away from three defenders on a 30-yard diagonal run. Rovers' full-back Gary Cooper managed to get a light grip on the youngster and then he was gone, speeding away for a brilliant twenty-fifth minute try goaled by Peter Bateson. His second try was the result of being in the right place at the right time after a wonderful long distance strike had ripped Featherstone apart. Bill Drake made the initial break from near his own 25-yard line, moving out to the right to get Stan Cowan away. The winger rounded his opposite number Cyril Woolford before linking up with Brian Cooper and when the centre looked for support there was Matthews to finish it all off in style.

Matthews completed his hat-trick in the last minute after Featherstone had threatened to snatch at least a draw, having cut Hull's lead to 10-5. It was a superb solo effort from a scrum inside Rovers' 25. Despite having to take Broadhurst's pass

---

Hull 15

  Tries: Matthews (3)
  Goals: Bateson (3)

Featherstone Rovers 5

  Try: Woolford
  Goal: Clawson

Hull centre Brian Saville slips a tackle to set up another attack.

from around his toes, Matthews was quickly into his stride to whip round Mullaney and sidestep Cooper to go in near the posts. Bateson tagged on the goal and Hull fans let rip with a full-throated chorus of *Old Faithful*.

Featherstone's fans drifted away quietly , wondering why their team had tried to take on the Hull forwards instead of relying on the football skills of the backs that had taken them to the semi-finals. Hull's pack was more than willing to take them on and some of the fierce exchanges finished with referee Norman Railton handing out warning lectures to players from each side. Both the Drake twins were laid out and there were flare-ups as their colleagues sought retribution.

Yet it could have been so different for Featherstone, who showed what might have been with the quality of their only try. It came in the sixty-eighth minute with Hull leading 10-2 and having rarely been under pressure. Scrum-half Alan Marchant produced a rare flash of his brilliance from deep inside the Rovers half before linking with Jim Hunt, who sent his winger Woolford streaking clear for a wonderful try. Featherstone had led 2-0 early on after Woolford kicked a penalty goal and were playing solidly enough until Matthews struck with his first try goaled by Bateson, who added a second half penalty.

In addition to highlighting Matthews' outstanding performance most reports gave full credit to Hull's forwards for laying the foundations for victory. Allan Cave of the *Daily Herald* wrote: 'Every one of Hull's redoubtable forwards hit his most devastating form. That is what Featherstone were up against. Is it any wonder they capitulated? The vision of a first-ever Wembley before their eyes inspired those fiery Hull forwards to one of their most glorious performances. I have run out of superlatives about Johnny Whiteley and company. One day I suppose Whiteley will surprise me by being merely brilliant!'

Hull: Bateson; Cowan, Saville, Cooper, Boustead; Matthews, Broadhurst; Scott, Harris, J. Drake, Sykes, W. Drake, J. Whiteley.

Featherstone Rovers: Cooper; Smith, Greatorex, Hunt, Woolford; Mullaney, Marchant; Anderson, Fawley, Jones, Hockley, Clamp, Clawson.

HULL v. WIGAN

Hopes so high, realisation so low. Hull went into their first ever Wembley final full of confidence and came away totally embarrassed after conceding a then stadium-record score. The ease with which Wigan won surprised everybody with match previews having predicted a battle royal. Wigan, who had finished second, were the slight favourites – Hull bookmaker Len Young offered them at 8-11 and the seventh-placed Airlie Birds at 11-10 – but it was all over by half-time as the cherry and whites romped to a 20-4 lead.

'Hull get the Wobbles' was typical of the headlines after the match and Tom Longworth of the *News Chronicle and Daily Dispatch* wrote: 'Never was a team expected to do so much, yet did so little as Hull. Even now, hours after the event, it seems unbelievable that a team considered to have a sporting chance of winning should have petered out so dismally as to have the highest score at Wembley registered against them. The tide seemed to be dead set against Hull from the first. If only they could have steadied their nerves they might have braced themselves to play as they know they can play. Instead, they fumbled and bungled from start to finish, positioned themselves badly, lacked their normal co-ordination and conceded six tries while only scoring one themselves. Wigan played almost to perfection, turning defence into attack in amazing fashion and leaving Hull with no counter.'

Most other reports blamed Hull's collapse on 'Wembley nerves' with one suggesting that it began effecting them twenty-four hours earlier on the traditional finalists' walkabout at the stadium. Hull's sudden change of plans meant they were still there when Wigan, who had the won Cup the year before and were making their sixth trip to Wembley, arrived and yelled at them to 'Get off our pitch!'. It is said that Hull shoulders sank and they never recovered their confidence. Even Hull coach Roy Francis admitted that although he did not believe in such things as nerves effecting experienced players he could think of no other reason for his team's inept performance. Yet the side was packed with experienced players, many of them having played in the three previous championship finals, iwhile Johnny Whiteley and Tommy Harris had helped Great Britain win the Ashes in Australia less than twelve months earlier.

It was the demolition of Hull's famed and feared pack that was the biggest surprise. Wigan clearly had the extra class among the backs with such all-time greats as Billy Boston, Eric Ashton and Mick Sullivan in their threequarter line, but few doubted that the Hull forwards would rule in mid-field. How wrong they were. The Wigan six were in control from the kick-off with Brian McTigue confirming his status as one of the greatest ever ball-playing forwards by winning the Lance Todd Trophy for a memorable Man of the Match performance. Bill Sayer even out-hooked Harris 17-11. Once Wigan's forwards had gained their early dominance it became embarrassingly easy for their much faster and classier backs to rip Hull to shreds with a series of long-distance strikes. Boston powered in for two tries on the right wing, Sullivan got another on the left, centre Keith Holden opened the scoring and stand off David Bolton also touched down as Hull's defence swung like an

---

Hull 13
   Try: Finn
   Goals: Keegan (5)

Wigan 30
   Tries: Boston (2), Sullivan, Holden
   Bolton, McTigue
   Goals: Griffiths (6)

Arthur Keegan kicks one of his five goals for Hull.

open gate. McTigue was the only forward to score and Fred Griffiths kicked a then Challenge Cup final record-equalling six goals.

Few of Hull's players came off with credit although captain Johnny Whiteley battled courageously in a long-lost cause. Midway through the second half he received a badly gashed head wound and rushed off to get it bandaged. He returned almost immediately with a scrum cap holding the bandage in place and did not have the wound stitched until after the match. No blame was attached to nineteen-year-old full-back Arthur Keegan for the record defeat. Completing his first season as a professional, the future Great Britain international had a hopeless task trying to hold back the Wigan attack as it broke through in waves. There were also no opportunities for him to link up in attack, but he did have some satisfaction in landing five goals. Four of them were from penalties to leave Hull with no complaints about referee Charlie Appleton. Hull's only try went to Tommy Finn late in the game, which despite Wigan's brilliant half-a-dozen touchdowns, was later chosen by BBC television to be shown with the credits at the start of their Saturday afternoon *Grandstand* programme.

The first trip to Wembley by a Hull club caused great excitement in the city and also some concern to the National Dock Labour Board, who feared the exodus of nearly half its force of 4,000 dockers to the match would bring the docks to a standstill. After refusing them permission to take the day off, a surprising number turned up for work on the Saturday. However, an estimated 20,000 Hull fans, including eleven train loads still invaded the capital, and all were in carnival mood

---

Hull: Keegan; Cowan, Cooper, Saville, Watts; Matthews, Finn; Scott, Harris, J. Drake, Sykes, W. Drake, J. Whiteley.

Wigan: Griffiths; Boston, Ashton, Holden, Sullivan; Bolton, Thomas; Bretherton, Sayer, Barton, McTigue, Cherrington, Evans.

– until the kick-off. One disappointment was that Hull were unable to wear their traditional irregular black and white hoops. The teams' colours would have clashed on black and white television and Hull lost the toss to decide who could retain their regular strip. Thus they turned out in an unfamiliar white jersey with a black V.

Within a few minutes of the two teams being presented to the Princess Royal (Mary) before a crowd of 79,811, who paid then record £35,718 receipts, Hull were making the first of their many mistakes. After only eight minutes they were behind as Wigan's two centres, Ashton and Holden, carved up the Hull defence with the latter leaving three defenders in his wake on a curving run to the posts. Griffiths added the goal and Keegan steadied Hull's nerves just a little with a penalty goal before Wigan had them reeling again. The Airlie Birds were starting to recover their composure and were showing plenty of enterprise when disaster struck in the twenty-second minute. They had Wigan under pressure in their own 25 until Finn lost the ball and Wigan's Bolton was on it in a flash. Before Hull could regroup the stand-off was haring off to halfway from where he sent Sullivan streaking clear for a spectacular touchdown in the corner. Griffiths banged over a superb goal.

Hull's only reply was another Keegan penalty goal for a scrum offence and then Wigan were back again, running in another try from 75 yards. The irrepressible McTigue did the early damage with a punishing charge before unleashing Bolton on

Brian Saville breaks down the left with Brian Cooper in support.

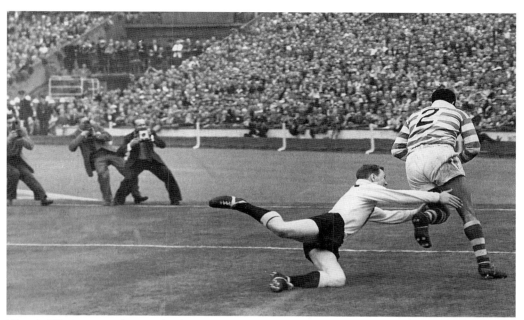

Wigan's Billy Boston strides out of Arthur Keegan's tackle for a try.

an unchallenged sprint from halfway. Griffiths tagged on the simple goal to make it 15-4 after thirty-two minutes. Worse was to follow before the interval as Boston virtually walked in at the corner after receiving a high pass from Bolton, who had wriggled through a clutch of defenders. Griffiths' goal gave Wigan their 16-point half-time lead. With Wigan having won the scrums 10-4, Hull hardly got a look in.

Hull improved a little early in the second half with Brian Saville and Brian Cooper both moving well before being smothered by Wigan's cover defence. There was even better by Finn, who made a good break from a scrum before he was brought down by Bolton. Hull continued to produce some improvement but all they had to show for it were two more penalty goals by Keegan before McTigue charged in for his try on the hour and Griffiths goaled. Wigan completed their try scoring ten minutes later when Boston won the chase to touch down Bolton's kick to make it 28-8. Finally, in the seventy-second minute, Hull got their one try as Finn took Jim Drake's pass and nipped round Griffiths for a try behind the posts to which Keegan added the goal. It was only the second try Wigan had conceded in the competition that season. But Griffiths put the bullet in Hull's head with a penalty goal two minutes from time.

Although the match was something of a horror show for Hull fans, it captivated Peter Wilson of the *Daily Mirror,* who was at the time one of the most respected of national sports journalists. 'I have only one prejudice against Rugby League,' he wrote. 'Why isn't it played constantly in the South? What a magnificent match the Rugby League Cup Final at Wembley was – the best afternoon I've spent at the famous stadium for months, if not years. These are the iron men of an iron and quicksilver sport. You'd have to have glue in your veins for your Adam's apple not to be bobbing up and down like a ping-pong ball in a shooting gallery. It is primarily the toughness at speed which remains with you. But, of course, there is much more than brute force and blinding ignorance about this magnificent "man" game.'

Hull v. Wakefield Trinity

14 May 1960   Rugby League Challenge Cup final
Wembley

A second successive record defeat for Hull at Wembley. This time though, there was no shame, only praise for their heroic battle against the odds. Hull went into the match without several first team regulars, including half their mighty pack, and were forced to bring in Mike Smith as the only player to make his first-team debut at Wembley. They suffered more injuries early in the game. Hull hadn't a chance, yet trailed only 7-5 at half-time and Wakefield Trinity did not score their second try against stricken foes until the forty-fifth minute. Then Hull's resistance broke and Wakefield piled up the then highest score in a Rugby League Challenge Cup final.

But whereas a year earlier Hull had been embarrassed by their 30-13 Wembley defeat against Wigan, this time the post-match reports gave them good cause to be proud of their efforts. Alfred Drewry wrote in the *Yorkshire Post*: 'Hull were the better side in the first half. Harris was the only forward on the field who could make ground consistently. What would have happened had the absent Sykes as well as Whiteley been there to support him is anybody's guess. Mine is that the Wakefield line would have fallen more than once.'

Tommy Harris's performance won him the Lance Todd Trophy as the Man of the Match. Hull's hooker gave the bravest performance seen at the stadium as he repeatedly broke through, despite suffering a succession of heavy tackles that left him reeling about the pitch before being led off with severe concussion twelve minutes from the end. Harris won the award by a record number of press votes – only one of thirty journalists did not select him – and sentiment had nothing to do with it. Although Wakefield centre Neil Fox scored a Cup final record of twenty points from seven goals and two tries, Harris had been the outstanding player for more than half the match. He lived up to his nickname of 'Bomber' by blasting big holes in Wakefield's defence – and won the scrums 15-10. Even the Queen, attending her first Rugby League match, recognised Harris's major contribution. 'It is amazing that such a small man can be at the bottom of a scrum and then be so active such a short time later' she was reported to have said to Rugby League Council member Bill Cunningham.

Hull's pre-match injury problems had intensified a week earlier when they lost 24-4 at Wakefield in a championship play-off semi-final. Peter Bateson, Hull's full-back and goal kicker, was ruled out of the Wembley final after being concussed by Wakefield's Derek Turner in an off-the-ball tackle. Hull picked up other injuries and did not finalise their line-up until the day of the match. In addition to Bateson, the other major absentees were the Drake twins, Bill and Jim, plus Cyril Sykes, while Jack Kershaw was only able to play after receiving a pain-killing jab for bruised ribs. The twenty-two-year-old Smith's shock selection meant that another reserve, Colin Cole, who had been in the second row a week earlier, was left out and he was so upset he refused to play for Hull again. But Nan Halafihi, a Tongan centre who had missed the previous seven matches because of injury, returned. He was regarded as Hull's lucky mascot as they had not been beaten in the fifteen matches he had played for them. Wakefield were at full strength apart from injured Harold Poynton being replaced by Ken Rollin at stand off.

Hull 5	Wakefield Trinity 38
Try: Cowan	*Tries:* Fox (2), Holliday (2), Skene (2) Rollin,
Goal: Evans	F. Smith
	Goals: Fox (7)

Mike Smith, who made his first-team debut at Wembley, is tackled by Wakefield's Jack Wilkinson.

Hull's worst fears seemed to be realised inside the first four minutes as a Neil Fox penalty goal was immediately followed by a try from Rollin, who broke through near halfway and won the chase to touch down after kicking ahead. But Hull refused to lie down and nine minutes later they were level after Stan Cowan twisted and turned for a stunning try behind the posts. Sam Evans added the goal, after Kershaw had missed with two earlier penalty attempts, and Hull fans began to think of miracles. Wakefield were now facing a much tougher game than expected, and gained some relief when Fox blasted over a penalty goal from way out. That made it 7-5 to Trinity and it stayed like that until half-time after Hull dug deep and raised hopes that they could achieve the near impossible.

The Airlie Birds were greeted by a chorus of *Old Faithful* when they returned for the second half, but Hull had already suffered further injury blows with Harris having treatment after being stretched out for two minutes and Cowan suffering a cracked rib in the twenty-fifth minute. Both battled on in the second half without being able to do anything to stop the inevitable Wakefield onslaught. The tries came thick and fast after Fox scored the first of his two touchdowns within five minutes of the restart.

Some were spectacular long-distance scores, with Hull players trailing in their wake, such as when Alan Skene swooped on a loose ball and sprinted 60 yards for Trinity's third try. Although Hull continued to go on the offensive, they did not have the same finishing power as Wakefield who finished with five tries in the last twenty minutes. They went to Holliday (60 minutes), Skene (65), Fox (72), Fred Smith (77) and Holliday (79). But the scoreline did not do justice to Hull's brave effort and they went off to a hero's reception.

Hull: Kershaw; Harrison, Cowan, Halafihi, Johnson; Broadhurst, Finn: Scott, Harris, Evans, M. Smith, Sutton, J. Whiteley.

Wakefield Trinity: Round; F. Smith, Skene, Fox, Etty; Rollin, Holliday; Wilkinson, Oakes, Vines, Firth, Chamberlain, Turner.

HULL v. FEATHERSTONE ROVERS

20 September 1969   Yorkshire Cup final
Headingley, Leeds

The Yorkshire Cup came back to The Boulevard for the first time in forty-six years after this tense victory over Featherstone Rovers. It was an extraordinary long spell without lifting the county trophy considering Hull had won the League championship three times in the same period. The Airlie Birds had been beaten in each of their eight previous Yorkshire Cup final appearances and there were times against Featherstone when it seemed they were set on throwing this one away. Although Hull were clearly the better side, a series of blunders cost them clear-cut scoring chances. None was more unbelievable than that made by Clive Sullivan, the Great Britain winger and one of Hull's most experienced players.

Hull were leading 7-4 well into the second half when Sullivan was given a golden opportunity to put them into a more commanding lead. Alan McGlone and Dick Gemmell set it up and Sullivan raced clear down the right, heading for what seemed to be his second touchdown. He crossed the goal line without a Featherstone player near him, but then continued too far into the in-goal and when turning to go in towards the posts he slipped and went over the dead-ball line. Sullivan scored a club record 250 tries for Hull, but this one he missed is remembered as clearly as the many great touchdowns he scored.

'My feet just shot from under me and I was out of play,' he said later. 'I felt like crying.' So did the Hull fans, but fortunately for Sullivan's peace of mind the Airlie Birds recovered and made almost certain of victory with a well taken second try. Gemmell and Joe Brown, the key figures in Hull's victory, combined superbly to create it. Gemmell made the initial break, flipped a back pass to Brown and the loose forward galloped clear before sending Jim Macklin in between the posts. John Maloney's simple goal made it 12-4 and that was a fair reflection of the game until Featherstone gave Hull an anxious last five minutes after Steve Nash nipped in for a try goaled by Cyril Kellett.

Brown took the White Rose Trophy as the Man of the Match and there is no doubt he had a massive influence, having a hand in both of Hull's tries and scoring their only first-half points with a drop goal, then worth two points. With McGlone winning overwhelming possession from the scrums, Brown also pinned Featherstone down with long touch-finding kicks in the second half. His all-round skills were highlighted in the fiftieth minute when he put Sullivan away for Hull's first try after regaining his own neat kick ahead. Featherstone fans howled for a forward pass to no avail. One mark against Brown was when he dummied through on a glorious run, but held on with support at hand and was brought down by Featherstone winger John Newlove.

Just how much Hull valued Gemmell's in their side can be gauged by their anxiety to get him fit for this one match. This was intensified when Arthur Keegan, their Great Britain full-back and inspirational captain, pulled out injured. Gemmell had taken no part in the Cup run and missed eight matches after injuring an ankle in the opening game. He was given a pain-killing injection to get him through the final and after an outstanding display as captain was not fit to play again for twelve weeks. Gemmell

Hull 12   **Featherstone Rovers 9**
Tries: Sullivan, J. Macklin   *Try:* Nash
Goals: Maloney (2)   *Goals:* Kellett (3)
Drop goal: Brown

Jim Macklin scores Hull's second try to the delight of Chris Davidson.

said the injured ankle was not painful during the match because he got a kick on it early on and it went numb. There had been much pre-match speculation whether the Great Britain centre would play and it looked a big gamble when he led the team out with an ankle covered in white strapping. But he said it was his 'good' ankle that was strapped to fool the opposition should they decide to give it an extra twist in the tackle.

Keegan did not miss many matches in his thirteen-year career with Hull and it is ironic that the only time they won a Cup final during his time at the club he was unable to play. His place was taken by Malcolm Owbridge, a youngster playing in only his seventh senior game. Reaching the final was obviously a surprise to Chris Forster because the second row forward had planned his wedding for the same day. It still went ahead and a few hours later Forster held nothing back in a hard-working performance.

Rugby league was going through a depression at the time and this was reflected in a crowd of only 11,089, which was the lowest to watch Hull in their seventeen Yorkshire Cup final appearances. Coached by former playing idol Johnny Whiteley, Hull had started slight favourites, being twelfth after ten matches in the thirty-club table with Featherstone three places below. The match was played under the four tackles and then a scrum rule, which had been brought in three years earlier, and Hull were given a big advantage by McGlone's hooking superiority. However, they wasted much of the possession by over-elaborating their attacks and losing the ball. Featherstone played a slower, more methodical game and were happy to take a 4-2 half-time lead thanks to two penalty goals by Cyril Kellett. Hull continued to miss chances in the second half, but made two count and the tries by Sullivan and Jim Macklin gave them a deserved victory.

Hull: Owbridge; Sullivan, Gemmell, Maloney, A. Macklin; Hancock, C. Davidson; Harrison, McGlone, J. Macklin, Kirchin, Forster, Brown.

Featherstone Rovers: C. Kellett; Newlove, Jordan, M. Smith, Hartley; D. Kellett, Nash; Tonks, Farrar, Lyons, A. Morgan, Thompson, Smales. Playing sub: Hudson.

Hull v. Leeds

10 September 1974
The Boulevard, Hull

Yorkshire Cup second round

Eleven Hull players pulled off one of the most remarkable victories in the club's history with this shock County Cup knockout. To have beaten the mighty Leeds in normal circumstances would have been an upset by a Hull side that was then a mediocre Division Two outfit, but to do it after having two players sent off before the interval puts it into the realm of fantasy. In an incident-packed game it looked at one stage as if some of Hull's remaining players were going to walk off in protest; a spectator jumped over the railing to get at the referee and Leeds also had a player dismissed midway through the second half.

Hull were leading 7-0 when the game exploded in the thirty-seventh minute and they were suddenly down to eleven men. It was sparked off by Leeds scrum-half Keith Hepworth's heavy tackle of Brian Hancock, which led to a scuffle between the half-backs. After they were pulled apart Hancock then kicked out at his opponents and was sent off by referee Eric Lawrinson, who was immediately surrounded by protesting Hull players. Len Casey obviously went a little further and was sent off for dissent. That seemed to be too much for Jim Macklin who led a group of Hull players in what appeared to be a walk off until they had a sudden change of mind when Leeds went on the attack. There was no further incident in the remaining couple of minutes of the half, but as the referee was leaving the field at the interval an irate fan ran towards him before being intercepted by police and led back. The referee then appeared to move in the direction of where the spectator had returned and was held back by Hull captain Chris Davidson.

Hancock, a clean player who had never been sent off before, was upset by his dismissal and said later: 'I was held by Hepworth and could not get up. When I did get free he threw a punch at me, but I did not really retaliate. I just tapped him with my boot. It was nothing.' Casey also pleaded innocence, claiming: 'All I said to the referee was "Come on ref"'.

If the first half was unsavoury, the second half was one to relish – at least for the loyal Hull fans in the meagre crowd of just 3,067. They got right behind their team from the restart and roared them on to heroic efforts, but surely the most they dared hope was that Hull would go down fighting. The magnificent eleven had other ideas and far from closing up the game to try to hang on to their 7-0 lead as long as possible they went on the attack. Whatever coach David Doyle-Davidson said to rally his depleted troops at halftime certainly worked. Within two minutes they had even extended their lead with a Chris Davidson penalty goal. Leeds looked rattled and twice had to scramble the ball away after being driven into their in-goal era, while Tony Salmon went close to scoring in the corner. Hull needed to take something from all their efforts and Davidson managed it with a drop goal. Now Hull were 10-0 in front. Their fans could hardly believe it!

The long odds against Hull shortened a little in the sixty-third minute, when Hepworth was sent off, but lengthened again when Alan Smith finally broke the gallant home defence to score their first try. When Phil Cookson charged over for another try, goaled by John Holmes, to make it 10-8 few reckoned Hull could last

---

Hull 12
Try: Portz
Goals: Davidson (4)
Drop goal: Davidson

Leeds 8
Tries: Smith, Cookson
Goal: Holmes

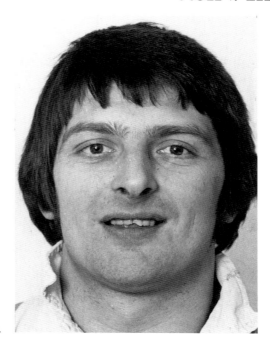

Len Casey, sent off for dissent.

out for another ten minutes. Somehow they did and even edged further ahead with Davidson's third penalty goal. The last few minutes became chaotic with Hull making so many quick substitutions that the referee stopped play to count how many players they had on the field. With that sorted out Hull's surviving players dug in once again until the final whistle heralded a memorable victory.

Leeds had held the Cup for two years and had been strong favourites to retain it. Their team was packed with internationals and coached by former Hull favourite Roy Francis they were to win the inaugural Premiership Trophy final at the end of the season, while Hull finished eighth in Division Two. But on this one night of the season they defied all odds and logic to pull off an amazing victory. In fact, even before they were greatly reduced in manpower Hull were rising to the occasion. They went on all-out attack from the kick-off and after Davidson had given them the lead with a tenth-minute penalty goal they stormed further ahead eighteen minutes later with a superb try. Hancock instigated it with a gem of an inside pass to send Steve Portz ripping through a series of attempted tackles to touch down behind the posts. Davidson tagged on the goal and Hull looked as if they were going to sweep Leeds aside until the double dismissal dramatically altered the pattern of the game and prepared the Airlie Birds for a glorious victory.

Dick Tingle of the *Hull Daily Mail* had no doubts about the magnitude of Hull's performance. He wrote: 'Hull FC's super eleven defied all the odds with sheer guts and determination. I doubt whether Hull have ever given a display to equal this.'

Hull: Stenton; A. Macklin, Portz, Crane, Salmon; Hancock, Davidson; Kear (Tindall), Duke, J. Macklin (Devonshire), Robson, Boxall, Casey.
Leeds: Marshall; Smith, Langley, Holmes, Atkinson; Hynes, Hepworth; Harrison, Fisher, Hicks (Cookson), Haigh, Clarkson, Batten.

13 November 1975   Players' No.6 Trophy second round replay
Headingley, Leeds

Brian Hancock totalled 107 tries playing in over 400 matches for Hull, and his greatest touchdown came in this most memorable of the stand off's performances. The match itself was also one to remember for the few faithful Hull supporters who made the Thursday night trip as they saw the Airlie Birds pull off a victory few expected after being held to a 9-9 draw at The Boulevard. Hancock set a magnificent captain's lead with a brilliant display that included a sensational 75-yard try and three drop goals.

Hull's shock victory was the first real sign that they were emerging from a depressing era and *Old Faithful* was sung more lustily than for many years. A new board of directors, including former centre Dick Gemmell, had taken over only a month earlier and coach David Doyle-Davidson was beginning to make his presence felt by motivating a mixed bunch of mostly average players into playing well above themselves. But they were still in the Second Division and a run of seven successive Cup and League victories did not include any top class scalps.

Then came the draw against Leeds, which was then deemed to be the height of their achievements. Leeds had also been on a winning run of eight matches, mostly against First Division opposition, and with their team of many internationals, home advantage was expected to give them a fairly comfortable win. The one thing in Hull's favour, however, was that Leeds were also due to face Hull Kingston Rovers in the Yorkshire Cup final two days later. They had wanted to play the replay a week later, but a Rugby Football League consultative committee ruled they must face Hull two days before the county final. It was to be a psychological boost for Hull, who made the most of it by storming into Leeds straight from the kick-off. Before then, however, they suffered a late blow when former Test hooker Peter Flanagan had to withdraw from the team just a few minutes before they left the dressing room when he got something in his eye. Flanagan had given Hull a big scrum advantage in the drawn tie and the pack reshuffle meant Keith Boxall switching from the second row for a rare appearance at hooker. Boxall was unable to give Hull the same amount of possession, but he had an outstanding game in the loose.

An added incentive for both teams was that the third-round draw had already been made and an attractive home tie against St Helens awaited the winners. But despite Leeds riding high in the League and aiming for their third final of the year, there were only 2,880 spectators scattered around the Headingley stadium when the teams took the field on a miserable November night. Although most of them were home fans their vocal support was overwhelmed by the Hull faithful who were soon in full voice acclaiming Hancock's wonderful try. It came after only five minutes with a suddenness that had Leeds reeling. Receiving swift service from a scrum inside Hull's own 25-yard area, Hancock shot out of the blocks to leave the Leeds half-backs grasping thin air. Approaching halfway, he sidestepped full-back David Marshall, outpaced centre Syd Hynes and just made it over the line as winger John Atkinson's desperate diving tackle brought him down near the posts. Mick Kendle added the goal and Hull were off to a flyer.

Hull 23
Tries: Macklin (2), Hancock, Foulkes
Goals: Kendle (4)
Drop Goals: Hancock (3)

Leeds 11
Tries: Smith, Pitchford, Dyl
Goal: Marshall

Brian Hancock, who scored a great try in a memorable display.

Leeds hit back within four minutes as the roly-poly Steve Pitchford barrelled his way over from short range in a repeat of the try he had scored in the drawn tie. Then came the first of Hancock's drop goals before for Alan Smith put Leeds level with the sort of try that made him one of the outstanding wingers of the era. It was a typical short, powerful burst by Smith as he blasted past four defenders to raise Leeds fans' hopes that the home side had got over their indifferent start and were about to put Hull in their place. In fact, it was Hull who responded in great style to stun the Leeds supporters into silence. Two penalty goals from Kendle eased Hull ahead and were followed by Ken Foulkes's cheeky try as the little scrum-half burrowed his way over from a play-the-ball close to the line. Kendle tagged on the goal and Hull went off at the interval to a rousing reception from their supporters who could hardly believe the 6-15 scoreline.

Hancock gave them more to cheer with another drop goal early in the second half before Les Dyl charged over to suggest Leeds were about to make a late bid for victory. Although Marshall missed for a third time with his goal attempt he banged over a penalty goal to make it 11-15 after fifty-two minutes, but that was as good as it got for Leeds. Hull came through a brief period of pressure to finish well on top. Hancock continued the agony for Leeds with the last of his three drop goals, which had acted like drip by drip torture. There was no question of Hull just hanging on for victory, however, and they finished with a remarkable flourish as local folk hero Alf Macklin whipped in for two late tries opposite Great Britain winger Atkinson. Macklin's outshining of the Leeds international epitomised Hull's victory as their team of grafters outclassed the aristocrats of Rugby League.

Hull: Kendle; A. Macklin, Clark, Portz, Hunter; Hancock, Foulkes; Ramsey, Boxall, Wardell (Salmon), Crane, Walker, Davidson.
Leeds: Marshall; A. Smith, Hynes (Hague), Dyl, Atkinson; Fletcher, Sanderson; Dickinson, Ward, Pitchford, Eccles, Batten, Cookson.

Hull v. Widnes

24 January 1976
Headingley, Leeds

Player's No.6 Trophy final

In Hull's long catalogue of heart-breaking Cup final defeats this one rates very high. The Second Division underdogs were given little chance of upsetting the First Division 'Cup Kings', but with only two minutes left Widnes led by only a point. Then the irrepressible Reg Bowden nipped in for the match-clinching try. It is of little consolation that all reports praised Hull for their tremendous effort. Twice they were being written off after trailing by eight and six points in each half, only for Hull to storm back to be level at half-time and almost upset the odds in the closing minutes.

This was Hull's first final of any kind for six years, while Widnes were aiming to pick up their third trophy inside ten months. Their strength was in a powerful pack plus a pair of influential half-backs, Eric Hughes and Bowden. They were expected to have too much big-match experience for a Hull side that was still mainly a team of battlers, who would fail to finish in one of the top four promotion places. But by sticking to coach David Doyle-Davidson's game plan and responding to his motivational speeches Hull worked themselves up for supreme efforts against the top guns. En route to the final they had beaten three of the First Division's major powers – Leeds, St. Helens and champions-to-be Salford.

'Widnes won the trophy and Hull took a winner's share of the accolades,' I wrote in the *Yorkshire Post*. 'It was that sort of a match. Both teams kept up an incredible pace right to the finish and showed enough enterprise to total seven tries despite the high standard of tackling. There was a period midway through the game when Hull's approach work reached great heights, but Widnes just held out and came back with their own brand of exhilarating attacking rugby.'

Hull had two outstanding individuals in Bill Ramsey and Mick Crane. Veteran prop Ramsey was particularly dominant in the first half when he combined with Crane to rip big holes in the Widnes defence. The pair linked in perfect harmony for Hull's first try, Ramsey slipping out a smart inside pass to Crane, who romped in after juggling to bring the ball under control. The ever-alert Crane struck again in the second half when he intercepted John Foran's pass to stroll over almost unchallenged.

Hull suffered a late injury blow when former Test hooker Peter Flanagan had to go off after giving them an 11-6 advantage in the scrums. Without him the Airlie Birds struggled for possession when they needed it most and Widnes won the last five scrums. Widnes's key player was their captain with Bowden taking the Man of the Match award for his impressive all-round contribution that included an early drop goal and a match-clinching late try. The sponsors were so impressed with Bowden's performance that they doubled his prize to £50.

The Player's No.6 Trophy competition, later to become the Regal Trophy, was in only its fifth season and the prize money was £6,000 for the winners with the losers taking £3,000. It was to become more popular in later years, but on a freezing January afternoon only 9,035, paying £6,275, braved the elements. They were soon to be warmed by a rousing match that was acclaimed as the most thrilling final so far.

A biting wind and snow flurries greeted the kick-off and pre-match forecasts of a comfortable Widnes victory seemed to be spot on as the favourites took a 7-0 lead

---

Hull 13

Tries: Crane (2), Hunter
Goals: Boxall (2)

Widnes 19

Tries: Jenkins (2), Bowden, Adams
Goals: Dutton (3)
Drop goal: Bowden

Mick Crane, scored two
of Hull's tries.

inside eight minutes. A Ray Dutton penalty goal got them off the mark and when he added the points to a Mick Adams try the gulf in class looked a mile wide. Hull also appeared physically inferior as the mighty Jim Mills had easily shoved off three defenders to send in Adams.

Bowden added a drop goal that extended the Widnes lead to eight points after less than twelve minutes. Hull did not panic and gradually heaved themselves into the game. After a brief period of consolidation they started to open out and surprised Widnes with their ability to keep the ball moving. Then came the defence-splitting manoeuvre by Ramsey and Crane that ended with the latter scoring between the posts and Keith Boxall adding a simple goal. There was no stopping Hull at this stage and they drew level before half-time with a well-worked try for Paul Hunter. If Widnes were rattled they did not show it and came out for the second half in the same confident mood that they had begun the game. Within fifteen minutes they were six points ahead after David Jenkins showed top-class finishing with two well-taken tries.

It was now 14-8 to Widnes. Surely they would start to pull away? They might have done had not Crane flashed in with his interception try and Boxall's goal left them only a point behind. Victory was there for the taking, but Hull could not quite grasp it. They started to fritter away possession, twice kicking aimlessly downfield, while back-chatting to the referee was punished by Dutton driving them back with two long penalty kicks to touch. But Hull were still in with a chance until Bowden came up with his gem of a try and Dutton added the goal. Despite the defeat Hull went off to a hero's welcome and from their dressing room came a chorus of *Old Faithful*.

Hull: Stephenson; A. Macklin, Clark, Portz, Hunter; Hancock, Foulkes (Davidson); Ramsey, Flanagan, Wardell, Boxall, Walker, Crane.
Widnes: Dutton; Prescott, George, Aspey, Jenkins; Hughes, Bowden; Mills, Elwell, J. Wood, Foran, Sheridan, Adams.

HULL v. NEW HUNSLET

18 May 1979   League match
The Boulevard

Played 26, won 26. That was Hull's record after this victory meant they finished the season as still the only club to win all their League matches in one campaign. They had already been acclaimed runaway Division Two champions and would finish nine points ahead of second-placed New Hunslet, who almost dashed Hull's unbeaten record in the last match. New Hunslet went into the match with an impressive run of their own, having won seventeen in succession since their last defeat – at home to Hull. Although the championship had already been decided, interest in the match reached Cup-tie intensity as the fans flocked to see if Hull could achieve the unbeatable record. And the fans set their own record with the Friday evening attendance of 12,424 still the biggest for a League match outside the top division.

Hull had also already set a Division Two record of scoring 144 tries but it was not until the last minute that they added to the total to clinch the all-important victory. Before that it looked as if they would have to scrape home with a seventieth minute penalty goal by Sammy Lloyd. But even Lloyd was well below his record-breaking best, having missed with five other shots at goal although the popular forward still finished the season with club record totals of 170 goals and 369 points. Charlie Stone, Lloyd's second-row partner, never went near records and scored only eight tries in nearly 200 appearances for Hull, but he grabbed the one that mattered when he crashed over in the last minute. Until then the big crowd had been held in suspense as Hull's 3-1 lead always looked vulnerable against a determined, if limited, Hunslet side.

Although Vince Farrar took Hull's Man of the Match award, their most dangerous players were John Newlove and Steve Norton. Newlove, father of future Great Britain centre Paul, was then at the veteran stage but still had plenty of class as a scheming stand off, while loose forward Norton produced the form that had made him one of the most idolised players in the club's history. One of Hunslet's best players was Tony Dean, who signed for Hull two years later and gave them great service in a brief spell. The wily scrum-half was noted for his drop kicking and he came up with a typical pot shot to jangle Hull's nerves when he made it 1-1 in the sixty-sixth minute.

Such was Hull's determination to finish the season with an unblemished League record, that coach Arthur Bunting rejected plans for them to be presented with the Division Two championship trophy before the match. 'Our aim is to win all twenty-six matches and I want nothing to take the players' minds off the job to be done,' said Bunting. 'Making presentations before the kick-off relaxes the players too much. I remember I was coach of Hull Kingston Rovers in 1975 when Huddersfield pipped us for the Division Two title. We played them in a Premiership match and after they had gone round with the championship trophy we thrashed them. I don't want that to happen today. The players have worked too hard building this record to let it slip now. They want to get into the record books and stay there because nobody can beat the unbeatable'.

Hull 6   **New Hunslet 1**
Try: Stone   *Drop goal:* Dean
Goal: Lloyd
Drop goal: Norton

Charlie Stone scored a late match-clinching try.

Despite Hull's careful preparations it did look for a long time that they might let the record slip from their grasp at the last moment. Hunslet refused to be mere record fodder and silenced Hull's usually vociferous Threepenny stand supporters for long periods with their tenacious tackling. On attack the visitors just kept plodding away looking for the vital breakthrough that never came. It might not have been exciting but it kept the crowd totally absorbed and in suspense right up to the final whistle.

Hull soon realised this was not going to be an easy night and after failing to make much impact against Hunslet's solid defence early on they were glad of the one point Norton snatched with a drop goal after the usually reliable Lloyd had missed with four penalty shots. Although Hull continued to do most of the pressing, their finishing was poor and there was no more scoring before the interval. Their 1-0 lead remained precarious and in the second half Hunslet started to pepper the goal with drop shot. Ian Cameron was off target with one effort and Dean with two more before he scored the equaliser.

With only twelve minutes remaining Hull began to look distinctly edgy as Tony Handforth continued to give Hunslet plenty of possession from the scrums, finishing with figures of 19-8 in his favour. It looked like ending in a stalemate until Lloyd finally found his best form and banged over a seventieth minute penalty goal that sneaked Hull in front. At 3-1 Hull still had a battle on their hands before Stone scored his last minute clincher. Now they could collect the trophy. In fact, captain Vince Farrar picked up two trophies as in addition to the Division Two Championship, Hull also received the Arrowfast Express Trophy and a cheque for £1,000 for scoring the most League tries in either division. Mention must also be made of the only two players who played in all twenty-six of Hull's winning matches – winger Graham Bray and Lloyd, the latter having the further distinction of kicking at least one goal in every match.

Hull: Robinson; Bray, Turner, Hancock, Prendiville; Newlove, Pickerill; Tindall (Lazenby), Duke (Boxall), Farrar, Stone, Lloyd, Norton.
New Hunslet: Briers; Muscroft, Parrish, Smith, Kingston (Barron); Cameron, Dean; Windmill, Handforth, Standidge, Hughes, Sykes, Griffiths.

HULL v. HULL KINGSTON ROVERS

18 December 1979   BBC 2 Floodlit Trophy final
The Boulevard

This was one of The Boulevard's most memorable nights. Hull Kingston Rovers were beaten in a Cup final before a capacity crowd – it does not get much better than that for Hull fans! A competition record 18,500 saw the Airlie Birds rise to the occasion to beat the reigning champions more emphatically than the scoreline suggests. Apart from winning the Division Two championship nine months earlier it was Hull's first trophy success for ten years.

Hull's victory was another big progressive stride towards the glory years of the early Eighties. They had been in Rovers' shadow for many years, but after gaining promotion as unbeaten champions Hull were already challenging them as the city's kingpins. Although the costly recruiting drive that was to make them a major power had begun a couple of years earlier with the signings of Steve Norton and Charlie Stone, Hull's side that faced Rovers was still basically a team of grafters and veterans. Yet they went into the final full of confidence after stringing together an unbeaten run of six matches and with Rovers also in top form the all-ticket match was soon a sell out. Many fans turned up on the night hoping to buy tickets and Hull estimated they could have sold an extra 10,000; all this despite the Tuesday night fixture being televised by the BBC.

Roger Millward, Rovers' player-coach, summed up the atmosphere when he said: 'Derby matches are tough anywhere, but in Hull they seem to be extra special. In many ways they are like Test matches. The supporters make it like that; both lots are fanatical.' Millward, in fact, missed playing in the final after having his jaw cracked in the semi-final defeat of St Helens and David Hall was brought in at stand off to replace him. It was a major blow to club and player, although Hall was to be one of Rovers' few successes on a night when several of their more experienced players failed to hit top form.

In contrast, almost every one of Hull's side played up to or above form with Paul Woods taking their Man of the Match award. It was a typical battling performance by the pugnacious Welsh full-back whose powerful rearguard running often changed defence into attack. There was no stopping him when he charged over two defenders to set up a try for Graham Evans. Rovers loose forward Phil Hogan felt the full force of Woods's determination and was carried off on a stretcher.

Hull also owed much to their veteran half-back pair, tall John Newlove and little Keith Hepworth. Newlove was coolness personified, while thirty-eight year old 'Heppy' was irrepressible despite finishing the match with a broken hand. The odd couple worked in perfect harmony from a scrum when Woods joined the act to send in Evans for his try. At the other end of the age spectrum, eighteen-year-old Steve Dennison had a night he would remember for the rest of his life after scoring a breakaway try and kicking two goals. The young winger's try followed one of several errors by Rovers as he kicked ahead near halfway, collected the ball on the bounce and raced away accompanied by a mounting roar from Hull fans. Dennison was one of only three local-born players in the Hull team.

Hull's victory was built on the domination of their pack, with captain Vince Farrar setting a magnificent example up front. They were also on top in the scrums,

Hull 13
   Tries: Dennison, G. Evans, Birdsall
   Goals: Dennison (2)

Hull Kingston Rovers 3
   Try: Hubbard

Keith Hepworth gets the ball away from a scrum, protected by Hull loose forward Steve Norton.

which hooker Ron Wileman won 14-11. The possession was vital as referee Billy Thompson ladled out penalties 16-4 to Rovers. Brian Lockwood, who took Rovers' Man of the Match award, tried hard to inspire his colleagues with little response.

Fitting the Floodlit Trophy ties into the scheduled League programme meant Hull were playing their fifth match in sixteen days and Rovers their fourth in nine days. Recent form suggested it was going to be a close game, especially as they had drawn 20-20 at Craven Park earlier in the season. Both sets of supporters were in full voice long before the kick-off and the match began in an intense, electric atmosphere. The only sign of crowd trouble came within a few seconds of the kick-off when a flare was thrown on to the pitch and blazed away near the touchline until removed by a policeman. Then came a loudspeaker appeal for fans to come down from scaffolding holding the television crew.

Although Hull dominated the first half territorially they managed only a 5-0 interval lead thanks to Dennison's twenty-fourth-minute try, to which he added the goal. Dennison also added the goal to the try by Evans two minutes into the second half to put Hull well on the way to victory. But a run of nine successive penalties got Rovers back into the game and Steve Hubbard grabbed their only try in the sixty-ninth minute after touching down Allan Agar's kick. Within five minutes, however, Hull clinched victory when substitute forward Charlie Birdsall charged through a mob of defenders for a try that set off the most rousing chorus of *Old Faithful* heard at The Boulevard for many years. It was a moment to savour and, ironically, the marvellous occasion proved to be the last game of a competition that had provided regular Tuesday night viewing for fourteen years.

Hull: Woods; Bray, G. Evans, Coupland, Dennison; Newlove, Hepworth; Tindall, Wileman, Farrar, Stone, Boxall (Birdsall), Norton.

Hull Kingston Rovers: Robinson; Hubbard, Smith, B. Watson, Sullivan; Hall, Agar; Holdstock, Tyreman, Lockwood, Clarkson (Hartley), Lowe, Hogan (Millington).

Hull v. Hull Kingston Rovers

3 May 1980   Rugby League Challenge Cup final
Wembley

This was probably the greatest sporting event in the city of Hull's history. Hull and Rovers at Wembley – unbelievable. The build-up to the great occasion gripped the city as nothing has before or since, and it was estimated that more than half of the capacity 95,000 crowd came from Hull. Both sets of supporters boarded twenty-four trains heading for the capital and the only evident rivalry was in trying to out-sing each other; Hull fans belting out *Old Faithful* and Rovers' retorting with *Red, Red Robin*. Thousands more travelled by car or bus. 'Last one out turn off the light!' read a hand-written sign on the main road out of the city.

There was little to choose between the two sides and the bookmakers made them evens while offering odds of only 11-1 against a draw. Hull had finished third in their first season back in Division One with Rovers four places below. Rovers were also seeking revenge for the 13-3 defeat in the BBC 2 Floodlit Trophy final earlier in the season. Although the national press journalists agreed it was a hard one to call most of them predicted a win for Rovers and they were proved right. Hull's Wembley jinx continued as they matched Rovers' one try but had three other touchdowns disallowed by referee Fred Lindop. Club record goal kicker Sammy Lloyd missed the chance of kicking them to victory as he landed only one of five goal attempts. He had five goes at placing the ball after Tim Wilby scored Hull's only try and was way off target when he finally put boot to ball.

Few neutrals begrudged Rovers their victory, however, as they overcame a sickening injury blow to their captain and key player Roger Millward early in the game. The Great Britain stand off suffered a broken jaw after being the target for a shockingly late high tackle by Hull hooker Ron Wileman in the thirteenth minute. Millward refused to go off and though his activities were reduced considerably he did bang over a 30-yard drop goal just before half-time to give Rovers an 8-3 interval lead. But it was to be Millward's last first team match as he retired the following season after receiving a fourth broken jaw in ten months during a reserve game.

Hull had good and bad luck announcements in the run up to the game. The good news was that Welsh centre Graham Walters escaped suspension when the Rugby League disciplinary committee ruled sending off was sufficient punishment for his last minute dismissal in the semi-final defeat of Widnes. But Graham Evans suffered the cruellest of late blows when he had to give up his substitute role after injuring a leg during a gymnasium game of soccer two days before the final. His place was taken by Brian Hancock, which was fair reward for a player who had battled through the bad times with Hull to share in the glory of this great day in front of 95,000 spectators. He was the only survivor from the team that played in front of a mere 983 at The Boulevard when Huyton were the visitors only five years earlier. Although Hull had little luck during the game the three no-try decisions that went against them in the second half all proved to be right when viewed later on video. In fact, Hull and Lloyd in particular had only themselves to blame for the first disallowed touchdown. Hull flashed the ball across field in brilliant style for

---

Hull 5
Try: Wilby
Goal: Lloyd

Hull Kingston Rovers 10
Try: Hubbard
Goals: Hubbard (3)
Drop goal: Millward

John Newlove moves across to link with Tim Wilby.

Graham Bray to be given a big overlap on the right and he was running round to the posts when the whistle went for an unnecessary obstruction by Lloyd. A try and goal then would have put Hull level at 8-8 and a little later Keith Tindall seemed to be on his way for a try after breaking a tackle only for Steve Norton's pass to be ruled forward. Then Wileman burrowed in from a play-the-ball but was unable to get the ball down in a three-man tackle. So near yet so far was the story of the match for Hull. Rovers could also point to a couple of disallowed touchdowns, a forward pass preventing Steve Hartley scoring between the posts and Steve Hubbard clearly making a double movement when reaching out for what would have been his second try. Hubbard still made a major contribution to Rovers' victory as he scored all but one of their ten points from a try and three penalty goals.

But the Lance Todd Trophy went to Brian Lockwood for his Man of the Match performance, which included the well-timed pass that sent Hubbard away for Rovers' only try. Hull's best was Norton, who led the side in great style, while club captain Vince Farrar remained on the substitutes' bench until the seventy-first minute. Lloyd also ran strongly in the second row, although he was in tears after the match because of his rare goal kicking lapses. With the scrums levelled at 8-8, Rovers had an 18-14 penalty count advantage in a game that was far from being a classic but was packed with tension and was in doubt right up to the last whistle, which came with Hull pressing strongly to snatch a draw.

The *Sunday Telegraph*'s Michael Crossley summed up the view of most neutrals when he wrote: 'Sadly, the match fell far short of expectations. Over familiarity of

---

Hull: Woods; Bray, Walters, Wilby, Prendiville; Newlove (Hancock), Pickerill; Tindall, Wileman, Stone (Farrar), Lloyd, Birdsall, Norton.

Hull Kingston Rovers: Hall; Hubbard (Hogan), Smith, Hartley, Sullivan; Millward, Agar; Holdstock, Watkinson, Lockwood, Lowe, Rose (Millington), Casey.

these neighbours made them almost completely cancel each other out. Clean breaks were a rarity and the flow of action was not aided by a succession of penalties and, the blight of the game, untidy scrimmaging which the referee never solved'.

Rovers' Allan Agar kicked off the historic match with Hull defending the players' tunnel end. Woods fielded the ball safely and the pattern for the match was set as Hull barged forward through the first two sets of play before cautiously opening out a little. Rovers replied in similar style, but they looked a little more confident from the start and went 7-0 up inside fifteen minutes. They opened the scoring with Hubbard's eighth-minute try from a tap penalty after Millward had found touch 35 yards from the Hull line. It was clearly a well-planned move with David Watkinson, Roy Holdstock and Agar all handling before Lockwood delayed his pass perfectly as Hubbard ran across from the right wing and took the ball in full stride to score over on the left. Though Hubbard missed the conversion it was still turned into five points as a touch judge had reported a foul when the winger was tackled over the line. That meant a simple penalty shot in front of the posts and Hubbard made no mistake this time. The winger added a second penalty five minutes later after Stone was found punching Holdstock. Things were not looking good for Hull until they won a scrum close to Rovers' line and stand off John Newlove went round the blind side to send Tim Wilby crashing over in the twenty-eighth minute. Lloyd took an age with the conversion and was still well off target. Hull was right back in the game and finished the half strongly although Millward's drop goal nudged Rovers a little further in front.

The only second half scoring were penalties: Lloyd's one success in the fifty-first minute and Hubbard's third five minutes from the end. Hubbard was carried off on a stretcher a minute later after injuring an ankle, and as he departed Hull made a last desperate attempt to snatch at least a draw. They piled on the pressure and surged into Rovers' half, gaining ground rapidly before time ran out when Tindall was brought down as he charged for the line. Millward brought a wonderful career to a glorious end when he went up to receive the Cup from Queen Elizabeth The Queen Mother, and even Hull fans applauded their old Boulevard favourite Clive Sullivan as he collected his first Challenge Cup winners' medal at thirty-seven.

A disappointing irony was that due to a provincial newspaper strike the *Hull Daily Mail* was unable to cover this greatest of sporting occasions for the city until they brought out an excellent special eight-page broadsheet three weeks later. 'May 3 will be edged in gold when the chapter is written on Hull FC and Hull Kingston Rovers' finest sporting hour,' wrote Paul Williamson. 'Facts and figures will fade with time, but memories of the day Hull packed its bags and went to London will linger for ever. While history records the statistics, the spirit of 95,000 hopeful souls left to haunt the capital's sporting Mecca will remember the cheers, the tears and the heartbreak which made Wembley 1980 Hull's greatest magic moment.'

Hull hooker Ron Wileman moves in to tackle Phil Lowe.

Hull winger Graham Bray grimaces as he hears the whistle blowing for obstruction after crossing the try line.

Hull v. Hull Kingston Rovers

23 January 1982   John Player Trophy final
Headingley

A memorable 50-yard try by a hooker; two players sent off, including the victorious captain which sparked off a row; and a Cup final win for Hull over the old enemy. All in front of a then competition record crowd of 25,425. This John Player Trophy final certainly gave fans plenty to talk about for years afterwards.

Ron Wileman was the scorer of the game's only try and he never scored a better. His pace and determination would have done credit to a winger – for a hooker it was extraordinary. It was also exceptional in that defences were on top throughout the game and several much more talented backs could not find a way through. Hull were leading 2-0 in the twenty-seventh minute when Wileman shot away from a play-the-ball at halfway and went down the blindside close to the right hand touchline. Amazingly there was nobody ahead of him and he went straight as an arrow for the line.

'As soon as Mick Crane was tackled I saw that Rovers had left a gap near the touchline and I tried to hurry him up to play the ball,' explained Wileman. 'When I got the ball I looked up and there was still nobody there, so off I went. I think it is the farthest I have ever run for a try and as I got nearer the line I tried to count off the yards. I could see the cover coming across, but once I saw the line there was nothing going to stop me. Coming from a hooker I think it sickened Rovers.'

Ironically, there had been a doubt about Wileman playing after he had injured an ankle a week earlier and then aggravated it during a training session on the morning of the final. Although he was beaten 10-6 in the scrums the hooker had an industrious game in the loose and was one of several contenders for the Man of the Match award which went to Hull prop Trevor Skerrett. Hull's other prop, Charlie Stone, gained some notoriety as being probably the only captain to lift a trophy after being sent off. His dismissal, along with Rovers prop Roy Holdstock, came four minutes from the end of a typical fiery derby battle. Referee Fred Lindop said he sent off Stone for butting Rovers centre Mike Smith and then dismissed Holdstock for hitting the Hull captain.

With only four minutes left, Stone stood near the substitutes' bench and at least one Rovers official protested when the dismissed captain went up to receive the Cup. Rugby League secretary David Oxley said he could see nothing wrong with that and he was more concerned that several of Rovers players did not go up to collect their losers' medals. Oxley also protested to the BBC about the poor choice of recorded 'highlights' of the game on *Grandstand*. Some of the exciting moments they missed were two thrilling runs by Hull winger Paul Prendiville and another by Skerret plus a spectacular kick and catch by Rovers full-back George Fairbairn. Prendiville also made the tackle of the match when brought down Rovers stand off Steve Hartley just short of the line after a 60-yard burst.

An eighteen-year-old Lee Crooks gave an early indication that he was a player for the big occasion by kicking four goals and not being overawed by Rovers pack of internationals. All the goals were from penalties, as were Fairbairn's two for Rovers. The overall penalty count was 18-16 in Hull's favour, including 8-2 for fouls as the game hotted up towards its explosive finish. One of the penalties awarded to Rovers

---

Hull 12   **Hull Kingston Rovers 4**
  Try: Wileman   *Tries:* Fairbairn (2)
  Goals: Crooks (4)
  Drop goal: Dean

Ron Wileman, scorer of a memorable try, is closely watched this time by John Millington.

was reckoned to be vital – for Hull. It came late in the first half when Rovers piled on the pressure and looked set to score a try until Hull scrum-half Tony Dean gave away a penalty under his own posts. Fairbairn tagged on the goal but it was Hull who breathed a sigh of relief as it enabled them to stay in front and they reached the interval 5-2 ahead. 'It was deliberate,' admitted Dean, who popped over a drop goal to edge Hull further in front ten minutes after the restart before he went off with broken ribs four minutes later. The cheeky scrum-half revealed later that he had cracked his ribs in a match a week earlier, but kept quiet about it because he did not want to miss the final.

Rovers lost their scrum-half when Paul Harkin went off injured in the twenty-eighth minute and David Hall switched from loose forward to feed the scrums. They always looked a little disorganised after that and Hull gradually became more dominant. It remained mostly a forward battle with penalties playing an increasing role. Shortly after Dean's drop goal Crooks landed two more penalties to give Hull a 10-2 lead before Fairbairn replied with one for Rovers in the 65th minute. Yet another penalty goal from Crooks ended the scoring eight minutes from time, but the tension remained right up to the final whistle.

Open Rugby summed it up enthusiastically: 'It was a pulsating match that was a credit to the game. The lasting impression was the way the pendulum seems to have swung in the city of Hull. Only two years ago when the sides met at Wembley, Rovers were definitely everybody's 'good guys'. Now Hull have demonstrated just how it pays to concentrate on football.'

Hull: Banks; O'Hara, Harrison, Leuluai, Prendiville; Day, Dean (K. Harkin); Skerret, Wileman, Stone, Crane, L. Crooks, Norton.

Hull Kingston Rovers: Fairbairn; Hubbard, Smith, Hogan, Muscroft; Hartley, P. Harkin (Burton); Holdstock (Millington), Watkinson, S. Crooks, Lowe, Casey, Hall.

HULL v. WIDNES

1 May 1982   Rugby League Challenge Cup final
Wembley

This was the nearest Hull got to winning in six trips to Wembley. It looked as if they were heading for another disappointing defeat when they trailed 14-6 going into the last 13 minutes. But a tremendous fight back thrilled the 92,147 crowd and produced only the third draw in the Cup's long history. Even then the Wembley jinx seemed to taunt Hull as Sammy Lloyd's match-winning conversion attempt headed for its target and veered away at the last moment. 'I really thought I had won the match with that last kick,' said Lloyd later. 'I raised my hands to acclaim it and then the wind suddenly caught the ball and took it wide. I couldn't believe it.'

Nor could Widnes fans believe that their side had let the game slip through their fingers after scoring three tries to two. It looked as if they were heading for victory with every stride that Widnes winger Stuart Wright took on his 95-yard run for a try after intercepting Gary Kemble's pass in the sixty-second minute. Had Wright not taken the interception Hull winger Paul Prendiville would have walked in at the corner and it seemed as if the missed opportunity had cost the Airlie Birds the game.

But Hull, who had been over cautious until then, now decided to go on all-out attack. It paid dividends almost immediately as Steve Norton discarded his distributive role and decided to go forward on his own. Moving out wide in the sixty-seventh minute, the loose forward broke a tackle to charge over on the right. Lloyd added the goal and Hull were on the way back. Five minutes later they were level after eighteen-year-old Lee Crooks confirmed his rich promise as he slipped Eddie Cunningham's tackle and shot out a pass for Dane O'Hara to dive in at the corner. Crooks had only been on the field eight minutes after replacing Mick Crane and made an immediate impact. Although Lloyd just failed with the kick from near touch, it was his only miss from five shots, which was in stark contrast to only one success in five against Hull Kingston Rovers at Wembley two years earlier.

The contrasting moods in the dressing rooms after the game reflected how the game had gone. There was an air of dejection among the Widnes players as might be expected of a side who had just had victory snatched from their grasp. But Hull's players showed relief and optimism that they could carry on where they left off and win the replay. 'I think Widnes were lucky the final hooter went when it did,' said Hull coach Arthur Bunting. 'We were well on top then.'

Cunningham, the Widnes centre who was playing his first game in two months after recovering from a back injury, won the Lance Todd Trophy for a Man-of-the-Match performance that included two tries. But he also missed a couple of tackles that let in tries and Hull captain David Topliss was unlucky not to pick up the coveted award. The stand off was a constant threat to Widnes with his dashing runs and distribution, which included the long pass that led to Norton's try. Topliss came out well on top in his clash with Eric Hughes, who had played only three other matches at stand off that season and the pre-match assumption was that he had been brought in to mark Hull's chief play maker closely. In fact, Hughes had only been cleared to play in the final two days earlier after being found not guilty of a sending off offence. Hughes did not change his uncompromising style for Wembley

---

Hull 14
   Tries: Norton, O'Hara
   Goals: Lloyd (4)

Widnes 14
   Tries: Cunningham (2), Wright
   Goal: Gregory, Burke
   Drop goal: Elwell

Kevin Harkin sets up a Hull attack with Mick Crane in support.

and it cost his side six points from penalties plus a booking for a swinging high tackle on Topliss. Penalties overall went 10-5 to Hull with Widnes winning the scrums 11-10. Both teams had tries disallowed – Hull twice. Norton went through a large gap and was brought back for an obstruction and Terry Day was unable to get the ball down after struggling over the line. Wright claimed he had touched down for another Widnes try, but the video recording showed he had bounced the ball.

Although Widnes were the Cup holders, Hull went into the match as slight favourites after having beaten them 21-3 at The Boulevard in the final League match of the season a week earlier. But there was really little to choose between the two sides, with Hull finishing in second place just ahead of Widnes on points difference. Widnes hooker Keith Elwell was obviously expecting it to be a close game as he popped over a drop goal after only four minutes. Four minutes later Cunningham went in for the first of his two tries and Burke added the goal. Hull fans must have feared the worst, but the Airlie Birds tightened up their defence and with Lloyd banging over three penalty goals they reached the interval all square, 6-6.

The second half began similarly to the first with Cunningham charging in for another close-range try after fifty-two minutes and Andy Gregory, taking over from the injured Burke, adding the goal. Hull were in a real trouble and when Wright streaked away for his try the only consolation was that Gregory missed the goal. It was to prove a crucial miss as Hull stormed back to snatch the draw that was to lead to the greatest night in the club's history.

Hull: Kemble; O'Hara, Day, S. Evans, Prendiville; Topliss, Harkin; Skerrett, Wileman, Stone, Crane (L. Crooks), Lloyd, Norton.
Widnes: Burke (A. Myler); Wright, O'Loughlin, Cunningham, Basnett; Hughes, Gregory; M. O'Neill, Elwell, Lockwood (S. O'Neill), Gorley, Prescott, Adams.

HULL v. WIDNES

19 May 1982   Rugby League Challenge Cup final replay
Elland Road, Leeds

'Hull have won the Cup!' It was a simple opening sentence to the *Yorkshire Post* match report, but it said it all. After sixty-eight years and for only the second time in its history, the battered old trophy was back at The Boulevard. It was the Northern Union Cup when Hull last won it in 1914 and now it had the less reverent State Express sponsors' pre-fix attached. But to Hull fans it was still *The* Cup. This was the most memorable of nights for the club, and how their fans celebrated! *Old Faithful* echoed round the packed Elland Road ground long before the finish as Hull put their Wembley wobbles behind them and came up with one of their greatest ever performances. The drawn final had been an anti-climax; the replay left Hull fans wanting to see it over and over again.

Superbly led by captain David Topliss, the four-tries-to-one ratio emphasised Hull's clear superiority. Topliss was the dominant figure throughout the game, scoring two tries and having a crucial role in another. He was an obvious winner of the £200 Man of the Match award and was unlucky in that the Lance Todd Trophy had already gone to Eddie Cunningham's for his display in the drawn game. 'I've devoted my life to Rugby League and this is the happiest moment I can remember,' said Topliss, who had played in many finals and Test matches. 'I went through four months of agony with a leg injury earlier this season but tonight made it all worthwhile.'

Eighteen-year-old Lee Crooks pushed him close for match honours with a display that confirmed predictions of a great future for the Hull-born forward. Crooks scored half of Hull's points with three goals and a try including the late five points that finished off Widnes in the seventy-third minute. The youngster showed big match maturity beyond his years when he seized the opportunity to romp in behind the posts from a play-the-ball 10 yards out. He then sent the conversion soaring into the massed bank of black and white fans, whose acclaim was close to hysteria. 'I always hoped I would be in a Cup-winning team some time in my career, but for it to happen to me when I'm only eighteen is fantastic,' said Crooks, who revealed that he had intended to go for a drop goal a split second before he went in for his try. 'As I started to move forward to get into position I saw a gap appear and I went for it. I was surprised how easily I got to the line.'

At the other end of the age spectrum was Clive Sullivan, who made his debut for Hull two years before Crooks was born. The thirty-nine-year-old former Great Britain winger got a surprise late recall for his first senior game in three months when Dane O'Hara failed a fitness test. He thus became the only player to earn a Rugby League Challenge Cup winners' medal with both Hull and Rovers, having been on the latter's side when they won the famous 1980 derby battle at Wembley. Another veteran to have the twilight of his career brightened by an unexpected big match call was thirty-seven-year-old Tony Duke, who had never played in a final during his fourteen years with Hull. The loyal, hard-working hooker was brought in after Ron Wileman was ruled out with an injury and justified his call up by beating Widnes international Keith Elwell 13-6 in the scrums. The possession was vital as penalties went 16-7 against Hull.

Hull 18
  Tries: Topliss (2), Kemble, Crooks
  Goals: Crooks (3)

Widnes 9
  Try: Wright
  Goals: Burke (3)

Gary Kemble strides in for Hull's brilliant first try.

In addition to the two enforced injury changes, coach Arthur Bunting, who must take due credit for the victory, dropped four other players from their Wembley starting line up. The key change was bringing in Tony Dean for Kevin Harkin at scrum-half, while James Leuluai was preferred to Terry Day at centre. The pack was given a more solid look with Keith Tindall and Crooks starting ahead of Mick Crane and Sammy Lloyd. 'We went to work after Saturday's defeat by Widnes in the Premiership final and came up with all the right answers. I admit we squandered a bit of possession, but we were determined to play them at thirteen-man rugby to counter their defensive skills and it worked a treat because we scored four tries.'

Widnes kept faith with their entire Wembley starting line up and Fred Lindop was again the referee. Hull's injury problems and the fact that they had lost 23-8 to Widnes in the Premiership final at Headingley four days earlier resulted in the favourites' tag swinging slightly away from them. But their supporters were ever faithful and created a fantastic atmosphere in a capacity Elland Road crowd of 41,171. They were still trying to squeeze them all in long after the kick-off and many missed Mick Burke's eighteenth-minute penalty goal from a yard inside Hull's half that opened the scoring. Spectators had spilled on to the field behind the Hull posts at this stage and there was an announcement for those in the stand to move forward as efforts were made to squeeze more into the ground.

Burke was off target with another penalty attempt and Tony Dean fared no better when he sought to get Hull off the mark with a drop goal. With Duke shovelling the ball out of the scrums Hull put Widnes under a tremendous amount of pressure and it paid off with two superbly-worked tries in the last seven minutes of the half. Both

---

Hull: Kemble; Sullivan, Leuluai, S. Evans, Prendiville; Topliss, Dean; Tindall, Duke, Stone, Skerrett, L. Crooks, Norton (Crane).

Widnes: Burke; Wright, O'Loughlin, Cunningham, Basnett; Hughes, Gregory; M. O'Neill, Elwell, Lockwood, Gorley, Prescott, Adams.

came from scrums inside the Widnes 25 and close to the right-hand touchline line. The first was sparked off by the ever-alert Dean, who took a quick tap when Widnes were penalised at a scrum. He flashed the ball out to Steve Norton, who linked with Topliss and he sent full-back Gary Kemble sweeping in for a brilliant try. Crooks added the goal and six minutes later Hull had done it again. Dean again delivered quick service from a scrum and this time Leuluai and Topliss combined for the latter to curve away for another wonderful try as Widnes were fooled by decoy Kemble's dummy run. Crooks hit the post with his kick but Hull were well satisfied with an 8-2 interval lead and went off to rapturous applause from their fans.

'My first try worked like a charm,' said Topliss. 'We tried the move twice at Wembley but each time Eric Hughes spotted it and snuffed us out. But tonight the defence was opened up and I was over.'

A succession of penalties put Hull under pressure early in the second half and Burke added a fifty-seventh-minute goal to one of them. A minute later Widnes were only 8-7 behind after a brilliant kick and run raid by Andy Gregory. Although Kemble brought him down Elwell moved the ball quickly from acting half-back and O'Loughlin provided Wright with an ample overlap to go in at the corner. Burke's kick hit a post and bounced out to leave Hull still ahead but about to face their toughest test. Their response was magnificent as they surged to the other end and Topliss struck a decisive blow when Norton sent the stand off darting over from 15 yards after sixty-two minutes. Crooks tagged on the goal and Hull were on their way to victory. Burke's second penalty goal in the sixty-fourth minute maintained the intensity before Crooks settled it with his late try and goal. Only then did

Lee Crooks clinches victory with a late try.

Captain David Topliss (left) and Trevor Skerrett parade the Cup.

Bunting make his one substitution, sending on Mick Crane for Norton with Terry Day staying on the bench throughout, as did Widnes's two substitutes, Tony Myler and Fred Whitfield.

As the game drew to a close Hull were awarded their first penalty for thirty minutes and Crooks took his time preparing for a shot at goal. He was off target, but the Hull fans hardly noticed as they were already acclaiming a famous victory. Never has *Old Faithful* been sung with so much passion.

Hull's Steve Evans, who had made a bit of Cup history at Wembley by becoming the only player to appear in a final after being on the losing side with another club earlier in the competition, now picked up a winners' medal. The centre was in Featherstone Rovers' team when they lost to Hull Kingston Rovers in the preliminary round shortly before he signed for Hull for a then club record £70,000.

There were wild scenes of emotion as Topliss received the Cup from Neil McFarlane MP, the Minister for Sport. Hull also received £14,555 prize money, but this one was all about glory and making up for many Cup final disappointments.

Hull v. Bradford Northern

2 October 1982
Headingley, Leeds

Yorkshire Cup final

The wealth of talent Hull had recruited in the early Eighties was in stark contrast to Bradford Northern's paucity of quality players as the two clubs prepared for this county final. Both had injury problems, but while Hull replaced one star player with another Bradford had to make do and mend. Nowhere was Hull's reserve power more obvious than in the forwards, clearly outlined by coach Arthur Bunting when he explained his welcome pre-match selection problems.

'I had four outstanding players for the back three positions and was still uncertain who to choose a few hours before the match,' said Bunting. 'I even asked the players what I should do, but in the end the decision had to be mine. The choice was between Lee Crooks, Paul Rose, Mick Crane and Steve Norton (each one was to play in the Test series that year). All had been playing well, but Norton had been struggling a little after injury. So I left out the world's greatest loose forward. That is not an easy thing to do.'

Bradford suffered a major blow when their scrum-half and key player, Alan Redfearn, was ruled out with a rib injury and Dean Carroll switched from stand off. That left inexperienced utility back Keith Whiteman facing Hull's imminent Great Britain captain David Topliss. When Tony Dean dropped out with a rib injury, Hull brought in the equally experienced Kevin Harkin at scrum-half. It was a similar story on the wings where Bradford were forced to play Steve Pullen, who had played only eight first team matches, while Hull replaced injured New Zealander Dane O'Hara with another Test player, Britain's Steve Evans.

The strength of the two sides was reflected in their League positions with Hull lying third off the top on their way to winning the championship and Bradford third off the bottom. Little wonder Hull were made firm favourites, but it was not until late in the game that they made their superiority count and then only after Bunting finally sent on Norton to work his magic. With Hull looking far from comfortable despite leading 8-6 Norton replaced Crane in the fifty-seventh minute and within eight minutes had put through Rose for a try. Crooks added the goal and Hull were on the way to victory.

Although Norton's late introduction had a significant impact on the game, Rose was a tremendous force throughout for Hull. He scored two tries, had a big say in another and repeatedly put big dents in Bradford's defence with his powerful charges; all this after taking a pre-match pain-killing injection for a rib injury. Despite Rose's major contribution to victory the White Rose Trophy for the Man of the Match went to a loser, Bradford's Keith Mumby. The Northern full-back won it mainly for a magnificent defensive stint, which included a superb tackle that ended an early rampaging break by Rose. The Hull forward then played the ball to himself and crashed over for the first try.

The attendance of 11,755, although modest enough, was the biggest for a Yorkshire Cup final for fourteen years and the receipts of £21,940 easily a record up until then. The fans got their money's worth as Bradford made it a much tighter match than most people expected. Both teams sought to bolster their scoring with drop goals, Crooks popping over two for Hull and Carroll doing the same for Bradford. The nineteen-year-old Crooks, who also kicked two placed goals, again showed maturity

---

Hull 18
Tries: Rose (2), Prendiville, Evans
Goals: Crooks (2)
Drop goals: Crooks (2)

Bradford Northern 7
Try: Whiteman
Goal: Carroll
Drop goals: Carroll (2)

Paul Rose, who had a tremendous game, tests the Bradford defence again.

beyond his years in general play. Bradford also had a promising forward talent at hooker where Brian Noble won the scrums 10-8 opposite Keith Bridges, whom he had understudied until Hull signed the veteran from Northern a couple of months earlier. An 11-8 penalty count in Hull's favour balanced the possession.

Another big influence on Bradford's performance was coach Peter Fox, whose mark was stamped all over the game as Northern drove in hard, snapped up opportunities and kept well on top of Hull in defence. It was a tribute to his team's efforts that Hull led 7-6 at half-time only after Crooks landed his first drop goal a minute before the interval.

Rose's first try had come in the eleventh minute and he set up the next for Paul Prendiville fifteen minutes later. Crooks failed with both conversion attempts and against the run of play Bradford suddenly drew level. Carroll got them off the mark with a one-pointer after half-an-hour and three minutes later Bradford ripped down the middle with the best try of the match. Impressive loose forward Gary Hale made the initial break before Whiteman backed up to race between the posts. Carroll's goal increased Hull's anxiety and the Airlie Birds sought some relief with drop goals from Crooks on either side of the interval.

Yet another drop goal from Carroll maintained the pressure on Hull before the cavalry arrived in the form of Norton, who soon sent Rose charging in for his second try in the sixty-fifth minute. Crooks added the goal and a penalty four minutes later but it was not until Evans scored a last minute try that Hull could relax and be certain of victory. Topliss then went up to collect their third trophy of the year, putting it alongside the Rugby League Challenge Cup and John Player Trophy they had won the previous season.

Hull: Kemble; Evans, Day, Leuluai, Prendiville; Topliss, Harkin; Skerrett, Bridges, Stone, Rose, L. Crooks, Crane (Norton).

Bradford Northern: Mumby; Barends, Gant, Parker, Pullen (Smith); Whiteman, Carroll; Grayshon, Noble, Van Bellen (Sanderson), Idle, Jasiewicz, Hale.

HULL v. AUSTRALIA

16 November 1982   Tour match
The Boulevard, Hull

'Glorious in defeat' is an overworked phrase but never was it more apt than on this memorable occasion. It must have been something special when many fiercely partisan Hull supporters regard a defeat as one of the greatest matches they have seen. Of course, to lose to the 1982 Kangaroos was no disgrace. They were to be called the 'Invincibles' after becoming the first tour squad to win all their matches, but Hull took immense pride in Australia coach Frank Stanton's declaration that they gave them their toughest game. Stanton had already paid Hull a huge compliment before the match by naming a full strength team just four days before Australia were due to meet Great Britain in the second Test. It was the same one that had thrashed Britain 40-4 in the first Test and he believed only the best was good enough to beat Hull and set a Kangaroos' record of twelve successive tour wins.

'The fact that we have picked our first Test side is testimony to Hull's challenge as League leaders,' said Stanton. 'I am aware of the tremendous support for the game in Hull and know they appreciate our style of football. So I hope we get the chance to show them the best. If Hull are prepared to join us in playing football we should see a great game.'

Hull were prepared and the 16,049 who packed into The Boulevard did see a truly great game. It was not always pretty and some of the clashes were ferocity personified with Hull's 'young gun' Lee Crooks seeking an early showdown with Aussie bad man Les Boyd. They were soon trading blows and others joined in as referee John Holdsworth struggled to keep a grip on the game. Crooks had already been penalised for a foul that left Australia captain Max Krilich lying flat out and the Hull forward was a little lucky not to be punished more severely. For all the fierce exchange there were only two major casualties, Hull centre James Leuluai suffering a broken jaw and Australia full-back Greg Brentnall going off with concussion.

A 14-14 penalty count suggests the teams were equally to blame for all the unsavoury moments, but they also had a fair share in the thrilling end-to-end rugby. The forward battle was a tribute to Hull's almost entirely local-born pack, who met the Aussie six head on and never gave an inch. Without top forwards, Trevor Skerrett, Charlie Stone and Steve Norton, Hull's patched-up pack included veteran Mick Harrison, who was playing only his second match since returning from several years at Leeds. Mick Crane took over from Norton at loose forward and won Hull's Man of the Match award with a superb performance. Crane varied his tactics intelligently and was always a danger with his probing runs. Veteran hooker Keith Bridges, who gave the Airlie Birds a big 13-5 advantage in the scrums, was the only forward not born in Hull.

David Topliss was the inspiration behind the pack. Even playing opposite Australia's brilliant stand off Brett Kenny, Topliss stood out with a vintage display that included Hull's only try, a cleverly taken touchdown after he lobbed over a little kick and beat a packed defence to the ball. The score put Topliss among the elite seven players who managed to score a try against Australia on their fifteen-match tour.

Hull went into the match aiming to restore British pride after the Australians had swept aside most opposition with ease. The Airlie Birds had won nine successive

---

Hull 7
  Try: Topliss
  Goals: Crooks (2)

Australia 13
  Tries: Grothe (2), Boustead
  Goals: Meninga (2)

The full Australian tour squad. *From left to right, back row*: Ribot, McCabe, Miles, McKinnon, Schubert, Grothe, Muggleton, Young, Bentnall. *Middle row*: Stanton (coach), Meninga, Morris, Hancock, Reddy, Boyd, Brown, Conescu, Price, Kenny, Pearce. *Front row*: Richards (trainer), Anderson, Mortimer, Ella, Rogers, Farrington (manager), Krilich, Rysdale (manager), Lewis, Sterling, Boustead, Murray, Dr. Monaghan (medical officer).

matches and were the holders of three trophies, but they had not beaten the Kangaroos since their first tour of 1908-09. The atmosphere was electric from the start and the exchanges soon became explosive. Australia looked as if they were going to carve Hull up early on, but after two or three slashing raids failed to produce a try it was the home side who took the lead with a Crooks penalty goal after twenty-eight minutes. Now Hull started to get more into the game and Topliss stunned the Aussies with his try just before half-time. Crooks added the goal to give Hull a 7-0 interval lead, only the second time the Australians had trailed at half-time on this tour.

But the Kangaroos bounded back after the interval and within five minutes of the restart had scored their first try. Australia's Man of the Match Peter Sterling, who was to have a memorable spell at Hull a few years later, set it up with a diagonal run to put Kerry Boustead over. Ten minutes later Australia produced a brilliant piece of play to score their second try. Wayne Pearce made the initial break with a long run down the left before unleashing Mal Meninga. The big centre tried to outstrip Gary Kemble, but the full-back brought him down with a flying tackle only for Meninga to shoot out a pass to Eric Grothe and the powerful winger dived over in the corner. Hull's dream was beginning to fade and in the sixty-fourth minute Australia went ahead for the first time when Meninga hit a penalty goal from 30 yards. The Hull crowd were still roaring their team on but they were quietened when the Kangaroos combined in great style to send Grothe dashing in for his second try and Meninga landed the goal from way out to clinch victory.

Hull: Kemble; O'Hara, S. Evans, Leuluai (Banks), Prendiville; Topliss, Dean; Harrison (Sutton), Bridges, Rose, Proctor, Crooks, Crane.
Australia: Brentnall (Lewis); Boustead, Meninga, Rogers, Grothe; Kenny, Sterling; Young, Krilich, Boyd, Pearce, Reddy, Price.

HULL v. FEATHERSTONE ROVERS

7 May 1983   Rugby League Challenge Cup final
Wembley

Hull have suffered many heartbreaks and disappointments in Cup finals, but never anything to match the depths of despair produced by this shattering defeat. They went into the final as champions, while Featherstone Rovers had just avoided a bottom four relegation place after finishing twelfth of sixteen clubs. Rovers, 33-1 at the start of the competition, were given 10 points start on the handicap coupon and Hull were 4-1 on to retain the Cup. The result was the biggest shock at Wembley for over fifty years.

Both teams scored two tries and Featherstone Rovers snatched victory with Steve Quinn's controversial penalty goal three minutes from the end, but even the most partisan of Hull supporters had no stomach to dispute the result. They knew Hull were the architects of their own defeat. With just over twenty minutes left they were leading 12-5 and Featherstone would soon be down to twelve men for ten minutes after Rovers captain Terry Hudson was sent to the sin bin. Yet it was Featherstone's younger and comparatively inexperienced side that remained more composed to grab an unbelievable victory with a converted try and two penalty goals.

Even the loss of injured scrum-half Kevin Harkin after only sixteen minutes was little excuse for their well below par display. In fact, substitute Mick Crane was one of Hull's best players after going to scrum-half in the second half. Harkin was carried off on a stretcher after being accidentally kicked in the head by opposite number Hudson at a scrum, and about twenty minutes later he was followed by Featherstone centre John Gilbert, also suffering concussion. Gilbert's injury was the result of a high tackle by Paul Rose, which earned the Hull forward the doubtful distinction of being the first player to be sent to the sin bin at Wembley. In the fifty-eighth minute Featherstone's Hudson became the second after he kneed Topliss. By sending a player from both teams to the sin bin and handing each side fourteen penalties no one could accuse Widnes referee Robin Whitfield of bias!

Many Hull fans did not have the same opinion of Jim Reed, the Dewsbury touch judge who later received several abusive telephone calls disputing his decision that led to Quinn kicking the late winning penalty goal. It was Reed who ran on to report Charlie Stone for butting Featherstone's Peter Smith and left the referee with no option but to penalise the Hull forward. Stone, a former Featherstone player, admitted the offence but said Smith had butted him first. With the scores locked at 12-12 Quinn stepped forward to glory with a well-placed goal from twenty yards out and to the right of the posts.

It was Quinn's fourth goal from five attempts, while Crooks managed only three from five with his two penalty misses both from reasonable positions. Although Quinn was hailed as the match-winner, the Lance Todd Trophy as Man of the Match went to Featherstone second row David Hobbs, who scored both of their tries to become the first forward to score more than one in an Rugby League Challenge Cup final. There was also a vital contribution from Ray Handscombe, whose 11-5 scrum advantage kept much valuable possession from Hull's classier back division. Two of Featherstone's backs were only seventeen, substitute Paul Lyman and stand off Alan Banks.

Hull were given an early warning that Featherstone were in the mood to upset the

---

Hull 12   **Featherstone Rovers 14**
  Tries: Crooks, Leuluai   *Tries:* Hobbs (2)
  Goals: Crooks (3)   *Goals:* Quinn (4)

David Topliss prepares to pass to half back partner Kevin Harkin.

odds when Hobbs crashed over after only seven minutes. The try came from a planned move as Hudson delayed his pass at a tap penalty before sending the forward tearing through a tackle and over the line. Quinn missed the conversion but added a penalty later to give Rovers a 5-0 interval. Hull were not unduly concerned and within three minutes of the restart they were level, thanks to a penalty try between the posts awarded to Crooks. The referee ruled Crooks had been prevented from touching down by Hobbs after putting in a short kick from a play-the-ball. Crooks added the goal and Hull went ahead for the first time in the fifty-fourth minute with a James Leuluai try near the posts. After Crane and Topliss exchanged passes Rose charged through before Leuluai took over to slip a tackle and finish off a brilliant move. Crooks tagged on the goal and then a penalty three minutes later to make it 12-5.

Hull's supporters were in full voice now and preparing to enjoy the expected points rush. It never came. A sixty-fourth minute penalty from Quinn edged Rovers back into the game and seven minutes later he made it 12-12 by converting Hobbs's second try after the second row ripped through Hull's flagging defence. It looked as if Hull were to be involved in a second successive Wembley draw and the last ten minutes were full of high drama that kept a crowd of 84,969 in a high pitch of suspense. Rovers thought Hobbs had landed a match-winning drop goal and were celebrating the score when referee Whitfield ruled the ball had hit a Hull player on its way over the bar. That meant no goal in those days. But Featherstone were able to maintain the intense pressure due mainly to winning four of the last five scrums and being awarded six successive penalties to Hull's one. Then came the crucial penalty goal that dashed Hull's Wembley dream yet again.

Hull: Kemble; O'Hara, Evans, Leuluai, Prendiville; Topliss, Harkin (Day)(Crane); Skerrett, Bridges, Stone, Rose, L. Crooks, Norton.
Featherstone Rovers: Barker; Marsden, Quinn, Gilbert (Lyman), Kellett; Banks, Hudson; Gibbins, Handscombe, Hankins, D. Hobbs, Slatter (Siddall), Smith.

15 October 1983   Yorkshire Cup final
Elland Road, Leeds

The sight of Mick Crane puffing away at a cigarette in the dressing room only minutes after the end of a big match was not uncommon during Hull's glory years of the early Eighties. Such a scene greeted the press after his magnificent performance won him the White Rose Trophy as Man of the Match in this Yorkshire Cup final triumph. With black, tousled hair and a cigarette drooping lazily from his lips, Crane did not fit the image of your typical sporting hero, nor did he make any pretence to be one. Crane loved his Rugby League but did not appear to take it too seriously. Asked about his smoking habit after the brilliant display against Castleford, the loose forward said: 'I smoke thirty a day and feel as fit as ever. I think I am playing better now than I have done for a long while.'

Crane had a special rapport with the Boulevard fans. They loved his laid-back style and Hull-born pride, which made him 'one of us', and he became something of a folk hero. But make no mistake – he was a top-class player, as he showed when running smoke rings round Castleford. He wafted through for one try, had a hand in another, dropped a goal and did it in such a nonchalant way he made it look easy. In miserable, wet conditions, most of Crane's best efforts in the first half were wasted as colleagues failed to hold his potentially defence-splitting passes. When he decided to go on his own in the forty-seventh minute, Castleford were left reeling; a little dummy, a big hand off and he was gone like a puff of smoke for a try that took Hull to an 8-2 lead.

Crane was also prominent in the build-up to Hull's last try, scored by Wayne Proctor in the sixty-eighth minute after receiving from James Leuluai. With just four minutes left Crane added a low-flying drop goal from 30 yards out that completed the scoring. 'That was just a time-waster,' shrugged Crane later. 'They are not really worth much these days.' Although Crane was a clear Man of the Match winner, a mix-up in communication led to Hull scrum-half Tony Dean being announced as the White Rose Trophy recipient. It was a pity the scrum-half could not have been given some extra reward, for he did have a very good game as did prop Trevor Skerrett.

Crane was in such a rich vein of form in 1983 that he was preferred at loose forward to the great Steve Norton, who moved up to the second row although injury ruled him out of the final. A nineteen-year-old Lee Crooks was in the second row to give yet another performance that marked him out as a future great, having already played in a succession of Cup finals and Test matches. Eighteen-year-old Garry Schofield was another star in the making, playing only his sixth match and his third start since signing for Hull. A year earlier he had led Hunslet Parkside to victory in the Yorkshire Youth Cup final.

While the match saw the emergence of one or two stars of the future, another was fading in the Castleford side. At his peak player-coach Malcolm Reilly was a truly great loose forward with a tearaway style; now he was a thirty-five-year-old prop who bravely risked aggravating a permanent knee injury in an effort to inspire his team. It didn't work as Hull kept well on top and forced him into uncharacteristic errors. Castleford went into the match as League leaders with only one defeat in

Hull 13   **Castleford 2**
  Tries: O'Hara, Crane, Proctor   *Goal:* R. Beardmore
  Drop goal: Crane

Tony Dean gets the ball away despite attention from four Castleford defenders.

eight matches, but fourth-placed Hull remained favourites to retain the county Cup as they were the side that had beaten them. It was an emphatic victory, too, 40-18 on Castleford's own ground and few thought they could match Hull's all-round power in the final.

The crowd of 14,049 was the best at a Yorkshire Cup final for fifteen years and the £33,522 receipts a record for the competition. Although Castleford had a slight 12-11 advantage in the scrums, and penalties went their way 14-10, they rarely put Hull under sustained pressure. Despite their limited possession the Airlie Birds always appeared to be in control and on one of their few first half incursions into the Castleford 25 they opened the scoring, Gary Kemble racing up from full-back to send Dane O'Hara over in the corner after eighteen minutes. As the rain continued to wash out many handling moves the only other first half score was a thirty-fourth minute penalty goal by Castleford's Bob Beardmore to make 4-2 to Hull at half-time. The nearest Castleford went to scoring a try was when Tony Marchant touched down Beardmore's kick between the posts only for referee Billy Thompson to rule offside.

Just before the interval Castleford's Gary Connell was sent to the sin bin for tripping Leuluai and was followed early in the second by Hull winger O'Hara for a foul on Marchant. While they were off Crane moved in for his try and Hull looked to already have one hand on the trophy. It was just a question of mopping up and they did with Proctor's try and Crane's drop goal. In retaining the trophy, Hull's two successive Yorkshire Cup final triumphs equalled the number of times they had won it in the previous seventy-five years.

Hull: Kemble; Solal, Schofield, Leuluai, O'Hara; Topliss, Dean; Edmonds, Wileman, Skerrett, Proctor, L. Crooks, Crane.

Castleford: Coen; Fenton, Marchant, Hyde (Orum), Kear; Joyner, R. Beardmore; Connell, Horton, Reilly, Timson, James, England.

HULL v. HULL KINGSTON ROVERS

27 October 1984   Yorkshire Cup final
Boothferry Park, Hull

An extraordinary County Cup final packed with incidents ended with Hull winning the trophy for a third successive season. Any win over the old enemy gives Hull fans immense satisfaction, but they went into raptures over this one after going through the agony of seeing Rovers race into a 12-0 lead with three tries in the first thirty minutes. The Airlie Birds closed the gap to four points by the interval and surged ahead with a wonder try by Gary Kemble just two minutes after the restart. Fielding a 50-yard drop out in the still visible soccer centre circle, the full-back loped away on a long curving run that took him round a trans-fixed defence for a glorious touchdown in the corner. Remarkably, Kemble had taken a bad knock in the first half that left with him double vision and coach Arthur Bunting considered keeping him off after the interval. His gamble to send him out again paid off as Kemble added another try in a brilliant second-half performance. Kemble was one of only three players who had played in each of Hull's three successive Yorkshire Cup final wins, the others being fellow countryman James Leuluai and Lee Crooks.

Despite Kemble's massive contribution to victory, the overwhelming winner of the White Rose Trophy as Man of the Match was Peter Sterling. The Australian Test scrum-half was overshadowed by Rovers' Paul Harkin for most of the first half before finishing it with a hint of what was to come. A neat little kick set up a try for Crooks, which with Garry Schofield's second goal suddenly put Hull right back into a game they seemed to have lost already. Sterling began the game as if he had been tightly wound up and as he uncoiled the effect was startling. His variety of kicks was extended to two raking touch-finders and testing up-and-unders, while he increased his work rate with ball in hand and covered well in defence. As Sterling increased the tempo Hull responded with all out attack and long before the finish they had run Rovers ragged to total five tries against a side that had not conceded one in the three earlier rounds.

For all Sterling's inspirational efforts, Rovers coach Roger Millward had no doubt which player had done most to demolish his team. 'Steve Norton was the best player on the field by a long way,' he claimed. I recall being one of only two journalists to vote for Norton as the Man of the Match because he was the one player to cause Rovers problems when little went right for Hull in a disastrous first half hour and then began to toy with the opposition in a runaway second half. Norton's patience was tested early on as his ball-playing skills were wasted. It must have been heart-breaking for Norton as Rovers swept to their early 12-0 lead. His reward came in the second half when he received full support from his colleagues. Norton's delayed pass put Kemble through for his second try and then he backed up to score one himself from close range.

Although the pace was fast and furious it was without the nasty incidents that marred many derby battles until late in the game when Hull's Paul Rose was sent off only ninety seconds after going on as a seventy-third minute substitute. The former Rovers forward had not touched the ball and made only three tackles, including the high one on Andy Kelly that led to his dismissal. Referee Fred Lindop waved Rose

---

Hull 29

Tries: Kemble (2), Crooks, Norton, Evans
Goals: Schofield (4)
Drop goal: Schofield

Hull Kingston Rovers 12

Tries: Robinson, Fairbairn, Hall

Fred Ah Kuoi races away from Mark Broadhurst's attempted tackle.

contemptuously to the dressing room and said later: 'I sent him off for illegal use of the elbow. It was a stupid thing for him to do and I was not going to let him spoil a marvellous game.' Rovers winger David Laws was sent to the sin bin in the last minute for making abusive remarks to a touch judge and the penalty county went 11-7 in Hull's favour to offset an 11-5 scrum deficit.

The crowd of 25,243 was the biggest for a Yorkshire Cup final for twenty-four years. Hull were the underdogs as they were fourth from the bottom of a sixteen-club Division One headed by Rovers. The teams seemed to be even further apart as Rovers scored three tries in a devastating twenty-one-minute spell. The first came in the ninth minute when Ian Robinson went over and then David Hall put in George Fairbairn before going in for one himself. But with Fairbairn failing to add any goals Rovers' overwhelming supremacy was not reflected on the scoreboard. A Hull victory still seemed out of the question until they chipped at the lead with a Schofield penalty goal followed by his conversion of Crooks's thirty-eighth-minute try.

Hull needed an early breakthrough in the second half and it came with Kemble's marvellous try superbly goaled by Schofield, who tagged on a drop goal in the fifty-third minute to make it 15-12. The Airlie Birds were flying high and there was no stopping them, as Kemble shot in for his second try and Norton grabbed another converted by Schofield. Hull's fans were in carnival mood and Steve Evans was cheered home like a Derby winner when he intercepted Hall's pass and sprinted 90 yards for a spectacular final touchdown. With David Topliss a non-playing substitute, twenty-one-year-old Crooks went up as one of the youngest captains of a Cup-winning side.

Hull: Kemble; Leuluai, Schofield, S. Evans, O'Hara; Ah Kuoi, Sterling; Edmonds, Patrick, L. Crooks, Norton, Proctor, Divorty (Rose).

Hull K.R.: Fairbairn; Clark, Robinson, Prohm, Laws; M. Smith, Harkin (Rudd); Broadhurst, Watkinson, Ema (Hartley), Burton, Kelly, Hall.

HULL v. CASTLEFORD

10 April 1985
Headingley, Leeds

Rugby League Challenge Cup semi-final replay

For sheer intensity, passion, excitement and incident-packed drama, this torrid, sometimes brutal replay, rates as one of the most memorable matches seen by the author. The first half in particular seethed with emotion and had the 20,968 crowd in a state of frenzy. It produced six tries from end to end non-stop action; ferocious exchanges; a brutal tackle that led to Hull's Gary Kemble being carried off on a stretcher; Hull coach Arthur Bunting ordered from the pitch and ended with a mass brawl as the half-time hooter sounded.

Hull led 22-12 at the interval and though there was only one try in the second half the pace never let up. On a night of several outstanding performances the Man of the Match award went to Lee Crooks, Hull's young captain who displayed leadership qualities beyond his twenty-one years. The ball-playing prop had a hand in three of Hull's four tries in addition to kicking three goals. Challenging him strongly for match honours was Peter Sterling, who turned in another memorable performance. In many ways it was a repeat of the Australian Test scrum-half's influential display in the drawn game when he took the match award. He even repeated his feat of scoring a try after following his own up-and-under kick. Castleford clearly recognised that Sterling was Hull's key player and he came in for some pretty rough treatment.

Even Malcolm Reilly, their veteran player-coach who had played only once before that season, sent himself on as a substitute to try to keep Sterling quiet. Although Reilly could hardly raise a gallop because of an old knee injury he went to loose forward and at the first scrum targeted Sterling with a high shot. Sterling was also knocked down heavily by Andy Timson and went off for treatment before returning to torment Castleford. But the worst blow was suffered by Kemble, who was severely concussed in a late off-the-ball tackle by Castleford scrum-half Ian Orum. When referee John McDonald gave Orum only a ticking off and penalised him, Hull fans howled in protest. But McDonald did send off Hull coach Arthur Bunting when he went on the field to have a word with the official while Kemble was being treated. Orum was later banned for four matches after he was cited and found guilty on video evidence.

Following Kemble's departure on a stretcher, Hull's fans began baying for retribution and Australian forward John Muggleton answered the call to leave Castleford centre Gary Hyde stretched out with a late tackle. Now Castleford fans hurled their protests at the referee when Muggleton only received a warning and was penalised. The tinderbox atmosphere finally brought an explosion when the first half ended with a brawl involving several players from both sides behind the Hull posts. It followed an extraordinary conclusion to the half, which should have ended as the hooter sounded. But a touch judge had spotted a Castleford foul a few seconds earlier and Hull were awarded a penalty. After they kicked to touch, Crooks tried to bring the half to an instant end by taking the tap kick and falling to the ground. He was immediately penalised for a rarely seen voluntary tackle and it was from Castleford's penalty punt over the Hull line that the brawl broke out. Once order was restored the referee finally brought the first half to a close. Tempers

---

Hull 22

Tries: James, Leuluai, O'Hara, Sterling
Goals: Crooks (3)

Castleford 16

Tries: Chapman, Hyde, Roockley
Goals: Hyde (2)

Lee Crooks falls to
a Castleford tackle
with Peter Sterling
in support.

simmered down a little in the second half with the overall penalty count going 16-11 to Hull.

The Kemble incident spurred Hull to a tremendous fightback after Hyde had scored an early try and goal. They drew level after eighteen minutes thanks to great work by Crooks, who got Kevin O'Hara racing in at the corner and then landed a magnificent touchline goal. Four minutes later Hull went ahead with Sterling's try converted by Crooks. With the tempo increasing by the minute, Castleford roared back and drew level when David Roockley linked up from full-back to touch down between the posts and Hyde kicked the goal. This extraordinary match took another twist a few minutes later as Hull surged back in front following more brilliant play by Crooks. The young prop again ran like a threequarter to link with Muggleton, who sent Kevin James haring for the corner.

There was even better to come from Hull as they went further ahead with another thrilling try. Inevitably it was Crooks who made the initial break to give James Leuluai the opportunity to show his own special brand of magic. The New Zealander took the ball in full stride and then did a little shimmy to leave Roockley rooted and go in for a marvellous try. Crooks added the goal to give Hull their 22-12 interval lead. Despite losing the scrums 11-3 overall Hull played more superb rugby in the second half without being able to break the opposing defence completely and it was Castleford who finished as they began – with a try. David Plange set it up with a run from his own half before passing inside to Tony Marchant. The centre continued in great style and then handed on to Chris Chapman, who had cut across from the other wing to twist and turn his way over the line. It left Castleford only six points behind, but Hull were not to be denied another Wembley appearance and they held out for a memorable victory.

Hull: Kemble (Topliss); James, Schofield, Leuluai, O'Hara; S. Evans, Sterling; L. Crooks, Patrick, Puckering (Edmonds), Muggleton, Norton, Divorty.
Castleford: Roockley; Plange, Marchant, Hyde, Chapman; Joyner, Orum (Sigsworth); Ward, K. Beardmore, Johnson, Wilson (Reilly), Timson, England.

HULL v. WIGAN

'The greatest of all Wembley finals', 'Rugby League at its glorious best', and 'Hull's amazing fight-back made it a match to remember'. All this and much more has been said of the fiftieth final to be played at the grand old stadium. However, for Hull players and fans it was just another Wembley heartbreak, summed up by coach Arthur Bunting. 'It's nice to be told we've been great losers, because we are entertainers. But today I would rather have been bad winners,' said Bunting, who was still awaiting a victory after taking Hull to Wembley four times.

The brilliant, breathtaking action reached extraordinary heights in the last sixteen minutes when Hull fired back from being 28-12 down to almost snatch an incredible victory with three wonderful tries before time ran out. This was Hull's sixth – and last – appearance at Wembley and it is as if they were fated never to win there. At the time Hull's twenty-four points were the most by any beaten side at the stadium. In fact, only four winning teams had scored more. It was also the third time Hull had scored as many tries as the opposition and still not won. Few winning teams have played better at Wembley than Hull did against Wigan, who equalled and were later to shatter the record of seven wins at Wembley. Hull also shared equally the record ten tries – nine by backs – scored in a Wembley final, but the failure to convert any of them suggests they really were jinxed at the stadium. Another Wembley record was the attendance of 99,801. This was an adjusted figure after the capacity had originally been set at 95,000. But such was the demand for tickets that the limit was raised and after all 97,801 tickets had been sold before match day a further 2,000 complimentary tickets were included in a later official total.

All the match reports praised both teams for what most agreed was the greatest game they had seen at Wembley. Even Stephen Jones, the *Sunday Times*' rugby union correspondent who is so often critical of all things Rugby League, had to admit: 'On paper it looked like an epic Cup final – on the pitch it was that and so much more. Wigan won a contest of pace and brilliance ...' And Frank Keating, the *Guardian*'s top feature writer, after comparing rugby union unfavourably, wrote: 'One's faith in rugby football as one of modern man's finest minor inventions was fully restored.' Rugby League's regular reporters were unanimous in their praise. 'It was a football feast,' said Paul Rylance of the *Daily Telegraph*. 'Matches of such mouth-watering potential so often fall flat but on this special occasion both teams surpassed even the wildest speculation as Hull's blistering finish almost caught flagging Wigan in the last breathtaking minute. It was a football feast and records all the way to give Rugby League the best possible fiftieth Wembley anniversary'.

Amid all the superb teamwork there were several outstanding individual displays, mostly from among the then record ten overseas players to appear in a final. Although Brett Kenny became the first Australian to win the Lance Todd Trophy, two of the Wigan stand off's fellow countrymen gave performances that would have won the Man of the Match award in many other years. They were Hull scrum-half Peter Sterling and Wigan winger John Ferguson, who had been flown back from

---

Hull 24

Tries: Leuluai (2), James, Evans, Divorty
Goals: Crooks (2)

Wigan 28

Tries: Ferguson(2), Gill, Edwards, Kenny
Goals: Gill (3), Stephenson

Shaun Patrick falls to a heavy Wigan tackle.

Australia after having played a major role in previous rounds. Kenny was all that Wigan hoped, and Hull feared, he would be. The Australian Test stand off slipped out passes from the tightest of situations and glided effortlessly through openings to score one magnificent try and have a hand in three others. Kenny's try was typical of

---

Hull: Kemble; James, S. Evans, Leuluai, O'Hara (Schofield); Ah Kuoi, Sterling; L. Crooks, Patrick, Puckering (Divorty), Muggleton, Rose, Norton.
Wigan: Edwards; Ferguson, Stephenson, Donlan, Gill; Kenny, M. Ford; Courtney, Kiss, Case (Campbell), West, Dunn, Potter.

his style. He seemed to be only cantering when Mike Ford put him away near halfway, but his beautifully controlled running swept him majestically past Hull full-back Gary Kemble on a curving run to the corner.

By the time Kenny had set up a forty-third-minute try for Shaun Edwards, he had already done enough to win the individual award, but Sterling almost grabbed it and victory from him as he refused to accept defeat. When Hull slumped to 22-8 down in the forty-third minute his immediate reply was to tear into the Wigan defence with a slashing 35-yard charge to within a few feet of the line before hooking out a pass for Steve Evans to score in the corner. And when Hull were still 16 points behind going into the closing stages it was Sterling who inspired the startling fight-back. He received terrific support, particularly from Steve Norton and New Zealand Test centre James Leuluai, the latter scoring two late tries that sent Hull's hopes soaring.

Hull's starting line-up included a then record six overseas players to appear in a final. They were New Zealanders Gary Kemble, James Leuluai, Dane O'Hara and Fred Ah Kuoi, plus Australians Peter Sterling and John Muggleton. The only Hull-born players were the front row of Lee Crooks, Shaun Patrick and Neil Puckering with Paul Rose in the second row. Scrums were still contested then and Hull's young front row did well to win them 9-8 to offset an 8-6 penalty deficit. At twenty-one, Crooks was aiming to become the youngest-ever winning captain at Wembley. Although Kemble was declared fit after missing the last eight matches, the full-back did not appear to have fully recovered from the shocking head tackle in the semi-final replay which had concussed and ruled him out of action for almost a month. Kemble's usually perfectly timed and fearless tackles seemed to have lost its edge, most notably when Gill stepped out of the Kiwi's grasp on the way to his long distance try.

After beating Hull 46-12 in a Premiership semi-final at Central Park a week earlier Wigan were made 4-5 favourites to win the Cup with the Airlie Birds offered at evens. It was that close to call although Wigan had a more successful League season, finishing third to their opponents' sixth place. Hull's five previous Wembley visits had been hampered by poor starts, but this time they shot out of the blocks and for the first time beat their opponents to scoring the opening touchdown. Crooks had got them off the mark with a second-minute penalty goal and nine minutes later Kevin James scored from Kemble's inside pass after Sterling had been involved twice in the move. Six minutes later Wigan were level when Kenny kept the ball alive after the fifth tackle for Ian Potter's long pass, to send Ferguson skipping round Dane O'Hara for a well-worked try. Henderson Gill added the goal and in the twenty-seventh minute Wigan shot ahead with Kenny's marvellous try. David Stephenson added the goal and though Crooks replied with a thirty-third-minute penalty Wigan finished the half 16-8 ahead following a spectacular Gill try just before the interval. It followed a long pass from Kenny that enabled David Stephenson to launch Gill on a thrilling 75-yard dash up the touchline, stepping out of despairing tackles by Sterling and Kemble for a great score. The black winger's wide grin as he looked up from his touchdown would remain a lasting memory for Wigan fans. Hull must have already been thinking about the Wembley jinx. The Airlie Birds had produced some excellent attacking rugby and shown little of the early nerves that had upset them on previous trips to the stadium and yet they were eight points down. Worse was to follow.

The irrepressible Kenny struck yet again only three minutes after the interval, twisting round Sterling to give Shaun Edwards a clear 25-yard run to the posts. Gill's goal made it 22-8 to Wigan and Hull looked to be heading for a repeat of the 30-13 thrashing they suffered when the teams met at Wembley in 1959. But Sterling

Lee Crooks on the charge, backed up by Steve Evans.

dragged them back from embarrassment by digging deep and setting up the try for Evans in the forty-fifth minute. There was still no sign of a major fight-back, however, and when the elusive Ferguson broke away for another spectacular try Hull fans started to fear the worst again. Gill added the goal to make it 28-12, but after fifty-one minutes that was to be the end of Wigan's scoring. Now it was Hull's turn to produce something special with three tries in twelve astonishing minutes.

Leuluai began the scoring blitz in the sixty-fourth minute as smart passing ended with Rose sending in the centre from close range and when the ever-probing Sterling put substitute forward Gary Divorty over ten minutes later the tension became almost unbearable. Two minutes later it reached cracking point as Leuluai broke through near halfway and raced away for a glorious solo try that sent Hull's fans into raptures. But with Crooks missing with one and Garry Schofield two of the conversion attempts, Hull could not quite produce the final winning touch.

HULL v. NEW ZEALAND

17 November 1985   Tour match
The Boulevard, Hull

One of the most infamous and sensational matches ever seen at The Boulevard completed the New Zealand tour of 1985. Most of the ugliness came in an astonishing first half when Easingwold referee Gerry Kershaw sent off five players, and Hull centre Garry Schofield was carried off on a stretcher with an ankle injury. Three of the dismissed players were Kiwis, but after trailing 10-6 at half-time the tourists' ten men scored another twenty-seven points without reply. Although the second half was much calmer that, too, was marred by a brief brawl. This time the referee handed out only a general warning.

Four of the dismissed players went off in pairs. The first two to go were Hull's Lee Crooks and Kiwi scrum-half Clayton Friend after they had exchanged punches in the eleventh minute. They were followed by the opposing hookers, Hull's Shaun Patrick and Kiwi Howie Tamati, for fighting at a scrum just before half-time and in first half injury time New Zealand lost their other half-back when Olsen Filipaina was dismissed for dangerous kicking.

Immediately after the game, English League chairman Joe Seddon and New Zealand tour manager Jim Campbell acted as a disciplinary committee. They found all five players guilty, but ruled sending off was sufficient punishment in each case. Both coaches and some reports suggested it had not been an unduly dirty game and that the schoolmaster referee had overreacted. The match official also gained a little notoriety after being greeted with headlines of 'Kershaw's Law' following his post match explanation for the dismissals. 'As you gain experience you sense an atmosphere at games and I got a gut feeling about this one,' he said. 'I know that if I had not taken a strong line then the paying public would not have got their money's worth. It was Kershaw's Law that won the day in the second half when we saw the New Zealanders display some fine footballing skills without foul play. It was up to me to guarantee that the game would not become a series of fist fights and brawls. If I had not taken the action, I would have been crucified.'

In fact, he came in for strong criticism anyway. New Zealand coach Graham Lowe said: 'It was ridiculous. The main ingredient missing today was common sense.' His Hull counterpart, Arthur Bunting added: 'The game promised so much but ended up being a damp squib and it was the supporters who suffered.' The match came only a week after New Zealand had been involved in a mass third Test brawl with Great Britain and Bunting had predicted: 'I think this will be a very physical battle. I saw the Test match and thought the Kiwis went a little over the top. We'll meet strength with strength, but we are a very disciplined side and I don't expect it to get out of hand.'

Bunting also thought the inclusion of three New Zealand Test players in Hull's squad would give the fixture added bite as they would be playing opposite players out to displace them for the Tests in France. The three Hull Kiwis were Gary Kemble, James Leuluai and Dane O'Hara, while Fred Ah Kuoi was ruled out after being injured in the final Test. There could also have been a little fall out from the bitterly-fought third Test match with Schofield and Crooks again facing their Kiwi

Hull 10
  Try: Schofield

  Goals: Schofield, Crooks, Hick,

New Zealand 33
  Tries: Bourneville (2), Elia (2), Crequer,
      McGahan
  Goals: Wright (3), Filipaina
  Drop goal: Wright

Lee Crooks, pictured with ball, was sent off after only 11 minutes.

foes. Both had played major roles in foiling New Zealand's hopes of winning the series.

Whatever the reason for the outbursts of fighting, there is no doubt both teams were fired up and treated the 8,406 crowd to some early fiery exchanges. A fourth-minute penalty goal from Crooks gave Hull the lead after four minutes and they looked the better side in the opening stages with Australian forward Geoff Gerard leading Hull's midfield dominance. Then came the dismissal of Crooks and Friend as a little more bitterness crept into the game. Schofield's try came in the twenty-fifth minute when he won the race to touch down Steve Evans's kick and added the goal. But just a couple of minutes later Schofield fell awkwardly and was carried off to be replaced by teenager Steve Hick, who also took over the goal kicking and landed a penalty to make it 10-0.

The last six minutes of the first half had the crowd in a frenzy as Patrick and Tamati were sent off followed by Filipaina, who had just converted a Mark Elia try that started New Zealand's comeback. Hull's eleven men against New Zealand's ten produced an unreal match in the second half, but at least it produced plenty of open rugby. Most of it came from the tourists who went on all-out attack. Elia went in for his second try, Mark Bourneville also got a couple and there was one each for Hugh McGahan and Marty Crequer. Owen Wright banged over four goals, including a drop goal, to complete New Zealand's comprehensive victory.

Although the brawling and five dismissals resulted in some lurid headlines and bad press for Rugby League, both club and country escaped without any severe reprimand. The game has since passed into Boulevard folklore with stories of the game varying from 'It was a blood bath' to 'I don't know what all the fuss was about.'

Hull: Kemble; Eastwood, Schofield (Hick), Leuluai, O'Hara; S. Evans, Gascoigne; Gerard, Patrick, Puckering, Muggleton, L. Crooks, Divorty.

New Zealand: Williams; Bourneville, Bell, Elia, Crequer; Filipaina, Friend; Wright, H. Tamati, Goulding (Shelford), McGahan, Stewart, O'Regan (Cooper).

HULL v. WIDNES

12 May 1991   Premiership final
Old Trafford, Manchester

After disappointing in so many major finals when much was expected of them, Hull won the Premiership Trophy for the only time against all expectations. The shock defeat of hot favourites Widnes, who were aiming for a fourth successive Premiership final victory, must go down as one of Hull's greatest triumphs. It remained their only success in five Premiership finals. The Airlie Birds had already caused some surprise by finishing third after starting at 20-1 to win the championship, but despite Premiership impressive home wins over St Helens and Leeds few gave them much chance against Widnes. The Cheshire side had finished second, six points clear of Hull, and were regarded as one of the greatest teams of the last twenty years or so with several world-class players, including Martin Offiah and Jonathan Davies. It was generally thought that Hull's hard, grafting style would keep the game close for about an hour before Widnes's class took them clear.

In fact, Hull dominated almost throughout and finished emphatic winners after scoring three tries to one. They stuck religiously to the game plan and still managed to add a touch of flair that took Widnes by surprise. The match-clinching try came ten minutes from the end and was scored by Gary Nolan, who epitomised Hull's underdog tag as an unsung substitute eager to snatch his moment of glory. The twenty-four-year-old former Hull Dockers centre had signed for Hull six weeks earlier and this was only his fourth appearance, having made just one start. Nolan had already gained a little glory by snatching Hull an even more dramatic semi-final victory over Leeds when he went on as a substitute and scored the match-winning try with just two minutes remaining. Australian stand off Greg Mackey provided the scoring opportunity then with a towering kick and he was the supplier again in the final, this time with a pass. Widnes had been enjoying their best period of the game and after trailing 8-0 had closed the gap to four points with an Offiah try after a spectacular 75-yard move. It seemed as if the predictions that Widnes would pull away in the closing stages were about to be realised. Then Nolan struck with his try twenty-two minutes after replacing Damien McGarry. There did not appear to be any way of breaching a massed defence close to the Widnes line when Mackey slipped the ball to Nolan. But he hurled himself forward with a supreme writhing effort and somehow reached one elongated arm through tangled bodies to plant the ball over the line. Hull fans erupted, Nolan was ecstatic and only Paul Eastwood remained cool as he banged over the goal from near touch.

'It has all happened so fast it still hasn't sunk in,' said Nolan, who might not have been selected had his younger brother, Rob, a more regular first team squad member, not been injured. 'It's really unbelievable. I have come on three times as a sub and scored each time. It was a fabulous pass from Greg Mackey.'

The pass was just one of many influential touches that earned Mackey the Harry Sunderland Trophy as the Man of the Match. Hull's Australian captain dictated play from the first whistle, spraying out passes, putting in kicks and constantly probing for openings. It crowned a season of high consistency for the irrepressible half-back, who played in all thirty-three of Hull's matches and rarely gave a less than top class

Hull 14   **Widnes 4**
  Tries: G. Nolan, Walker, Gay   *Try:* Offiah
  Goals: Eastwood

Damien McGarry slips past John Devereux's flying tackle.

performance. His influential display in the final was up with the best. He mesmerised Widnes to set up Hull's first try as he pointed skywards to indicate a high kick after the fifth tackle, then suddenly moved the ball away for Richard Gay to crash over for a stunning thirteenth-minute touchdown.

The foundation for victory had been laid and was built on with the expected forward barrage led by mighty props Karl Harrison and Andy Dannatt. Behind them French Test scrum-half Patrick Entat completed a dictatorial half-back combination with Mackey and even their underrated threequarters produced flashes of brilliance. Hull's defence was equally impressive. They swarmed all over Widnes's star backs so that Davies and Co. rarely got a running chance. On the one occasion Davies threatened danger he was bundled into touch near the corner flag, as were Offiah and Alan Tait.

Hull's first trophy success for nearly seven years was also a triumph for their coaching staff with the Australian duo of Noel Cleal and Brian Smith coming in for an equal share of praise. Although Smith had returned home four months earlier he left behind a sound basis upon which Cleal was able to forge a victory plan after

Hull: Gay; Eastwood, McGarry (G. Nolan), Webb, Turner; Mackey, Entat; K. Harrison, L. Jackson, Dannatt, Marlow (Busby), Walker, Sharp.

Widnes: Tait; Devereux, Currier, Davies, Offiah; Dowd, D. Hulme; Sorensen, McKenzie (Wright), Grima, P. Hulme, Koloto (Howard), McCurrie.

Jonathan Davies is caught by a flying Patrick Entat tackle with Paul Eastwood ready to lend a hand.

spending twenty hours analysing video tapes of Widnes, who had beaten Hull in three previous Premiership finals.

Speculation was rife before the match that Widnes's coach, Doug Laughton, was about to leave for Leeds and it proved to be true a few days later. Pre-match harmony in the Widnes camp could not have been improved either by stories that Offiah had asked for a transfer and that, too, was confirmed when he joined Wigan midway through the next season.

Despite their late personnel problems Widnes remained strong favourites to retain the trophy after piling up 88 points in disposing of Bradford Northern and Featherstone Rovers in the previous play-off games. They had also beaten Hull three times in the final over the past nine seasons, so few in the Premiership final record crowd of 42,043 were expecting what was to follow. Gay's opening try gave an early indication that Hull were capable of much greater things than many good judges believed possible and it was confirmed with a glorious touchdown in the twenty-seventh minute. Entat teased his way through grasping defenders as he went searching for support on the right. Eastwood provided it and burrowed in field before arcing back towards the right where second row forward Russ Walker took over to crash through for the touchdown. Widnes were 8-0 down and it could have been more before half-time as Hull continued to outplay them in all departments, growing in confidence with every forward charge that occasionally expanded to a flowing threequarter line movement. The trophy holders had not expected this.

Only Widnes's solid defence kept Hull out as Harrison and Dannatt battered their way relentlessly up field with Lee Jackson at hooker adding a few subtle touches to complete an impressive front row. Jon Sharp also provided plenty of class at loose forward as Hull raised the hopes of their supporters and stunned the Widnes followers into puzzled silence. It was not until midway through the second half that Widnes began to produce the sort of play that had made them such an exciting and successful team. Steve McCurrie was the biggest threat to Hull and the powerful loose forward went close to grabbing Widnes's first try with a great solo dash that Hull did well to blot out. Then Widnes came up with a wonderful try from deep inside their own half. This was the sort of long distance strike Hull fans feared. Kurt Sorensen made the initial break with a thundering charge before David Hulme took over to send Offiah flying in. It was the winger's forty-ninth try of the season and put him clear at the top for a fourth successive season. With Davies becoming more of a threat it looked as if Widnes's back-line pace was about to make a late sprint for victory.

They should have scored again a few minutes later but made a mess of a defence-splitting break. When Emosi Koloto broke through he had Darren Wright up in support and it only needed a pass to send him on the way for a try. But Koloto inexplicably ignored him and lobbed a pass the other way to John Devereux, who lost the ball as he was tackled. It was a remarkable let off for Hull and they wavered a little before regrouping and hitting back in great style. Only Offiah's speed prevented Gay getting clear after a strong run and well-timed pass by Sharp. It was end-to-end rugby now with Alan Tait and David Hulme held just short of the Hull line in quick succession. Then it was the Airlie Birds' turn and they made it pay off with Nolan's stunning late try. The match was not yet won, however, and the Airlie Birds had to produce some tremendous defensive work as Widnes desperately tried to hit back. They tried everything to break Hull down, but with their supporters now roaring them on the black and white barrier held. The strains of *Old Faithful* echoed round the famous football stadium in the closing minutes as the Hull fans acclaimed a famous victory.

Jubilant Hull players celebrate their shock victory.

Hull Sharks v. Halifax Blue Sox

8 August 1999   Super League
The Boulevard, Hull

Hull seemed to be heading for defeat and relegation disgrace when they trailed 20-0 with only twenty minutes left before they staged probably the most amazing comeback in the club's long history. After fumbling their way through an hour of slip-shod rugby they suddenly hit top form to rattle in four tries, all goaled by Robert Roberts to pull off an unbelievable victory. Having been jeered early on by their exasperated fans, Hull's players went off to a hero's welcome amid scenes of jubilation not seen at The Boulevard for many years.

Hull were already 18-0 down at half-time and it took some time for coach Steve Crooks's blistering interval talk to take effect as they slipped a little further behind in the second half. But Crooks said later: 'I still thought we'd come back even when we were 20-0 down. I'm the eternal optimist. I've never spoken to a team like I did at half-time. You wouldn't be able to print most of what I said, but in the second half they showed great determination and in the end got what they deserved.'

Hull went into the match with only three wins from twenty-fourth League matches leaving them at rock bottom in only their second season of Super League. They were dark days for the club. Australian coach Peter Walsh had been sacked earlier in the season after a string of poor results and Steve Crooks struggled to instil some improvement. A club record 74-16 defeat was suffered at St Helens and a week before meeting Halifax they were handed a 40-12 home thrashing by Gateshead Thunder. Ironically, Gateshead were to save Hull from extinction when the two clubs agreed a controversial so-called merger later in the year.

Only 3,461 saw Hull begin well enough, but miss a couple of clear cut chances before Halifax took the lead against the run of play in the fourteenth minute. Prop Paul Broadbent set it up with a tremendous run and from the position gained Halifax moved the ball out quickly for Hull-born centre David Hodgson to go over. Graham Holroyd banged over the angled goal and ten minutes later cut out Halifax's next try. The scrum-half dodged through just inside home territory before sending winger Nick Pinkney, another Hull-born player, racing between the posts.

Hull's approach work continued to cause Halifax problems, but woeful finishing meant they were unable to turn any of it into points. In contrast, the visitors made their less frequent raids count and Holroyd's growing influence became apparent again when he collected his own kick to score their third try. His goal was a formality and Hull slunk off at half-time to derisive shouts from their own fans. The second half began in similar pattern to the first with Hull showing some enterprising play only to waste all their efforts with poor finishing. They were lucky that when Halifax made one of their rare raids player-coach Gary Mercer had a try disallowed for a double movement in the fifty-fourth minute. A try then would surely have ended any wild notion of Hull being able to win the game. It still remained the remotest of possibilities two minutes later when a Holroyd penalty goal made it 20-0 to the Blue Sox.

However, the dramatic and sudden change of events began on the hour when Hull scored their first try. It was a superb one, too, with Logan Campbell surging

---

Hull 24
  Tries: Horne, Craven, M. Smith, Hallas
  Goals: Roberts (4)

Halifax Blue Sox 21
  Tries: Hodgson, Pinkney, Holroyd
  Goals: Holroyd (4)
  Drop goal: Holroyd

Steve Crooks, Hull's coach who
gave his team a half-time roasting.

down the left before passing inside to send Richard Horne bursting through full-back Daryl Cardiss's tackle for a try in the corner. Although Roberts added the goal it still looked like a damage-limitation score by Hull until they roared back with another terrific try. It began with Graeme Hallas ripping the ball off Mick Shaw and linking with Gary Lester on a 60-metre raid. The ever-alert Horne took over to send Steve Craven crashing over and when Roberts's goal left Hull only eight points behind, The Boulevard suddenly became a cauldron of excitement.

Holroyd realised the danger and thought he had edged Halifax a little nearer to safety with a drop goal ten minutes from time. But two minutes later the alarm bells were ringing louder than ever for his side when Roberts slipped out a short pass that sent Michael Smith barging over. Roberts banged over the goal and now Hull were only three points behind. The tension was becoming unbearable for Hull's fans, who were now totally behind their team. With less than two minutes left they thought they were roaring home the winner when Horne kicked ahead and won the chase to touch down only for referee John Connolly to disallow it. But the groans and boos that greeted the decision changed to delirious cheers within a minute when Horne put in another kick and this time Hallas scored the match-winning try against his old team. Roberts added his fourth goal with the last kick of the match to complete one of the most extraordinary matches seen at The Boulevard.

It was also to prove one of the most important victories in the club's history as Hull did not win again until the last match of the season when only a better scoring average enabled them to stay above bottom club Huddersfield. In fact, other events meant there was to be no relegation from Super League, but that could not alter the drama of Hull's astonishing defeat of Halifax.

Hull: Poucher; Parker, Campbell, Hallas, Baildon; Cooke (Horne), Lester; K. Harrison (Pickavance) (R. Nolan), King, Craven, Booth (M. Smith), Leatham, Roberts .

Halifax: Cardiss; Pinkney, Craig, Hodgson, Marns; Gibson, Holroyd; Broadbent (Hobson), Shaw, Marshall (Gillespie), Gannon (Clark), Mercer, Moana (Knox).

Hull FC v. New Zealand

22 October 2002   Tour match
The Boulevard, Hull

Farewell to The Boulevard! Hull played their last match at the famous old ground on a night filled with nostalgia and emotion. A capacity crowd of 12,092 produced an atmosphere that recalled The Boulevard's greatest days with *Old Faithful* sang at its loudest over and over again, especially by the Threepenny stand fans. There was even a mellow and bright *Old Faithful* moon shining down to light up a memorable occasion. The match also heralded the opening of the Kiwis' first tour since 1993 and the New Zealanders played their part with an entertaining brand of second-half rugby that brought an emphatic victory after they had trailed 7-6 at half-time. The Kiwis were fitting opponents, for New Zealanders had played a major role in Hull's last glorious era of the Eighties and one of them, former Test full-back Gary Kemble, played in the pre-match veterans' game of touch rugby which was part of the night's farewell celebrations.

When seventy-one-year-old Boulevard legend Johnny Whiteley led out the teams for the veterans' curtain-raiser, the emotion was palpable and the former Great Britain Test loose forward admitted: 'I felt myself filling up and even though I played in some great games I've never felt like this.' After some of Hull's greatest players of the past had stirred memories with their still admirable skills, albeit executed at a much slower pace, the stage was prepared for the main attraction. A simple but brilliantly effective touch was the parading of schoolchildren round the perimeter of the famous pitch, each holding a black or white balloon which they released into a starlit sky as the two teams walked out to thunderous applause and yet another chorus of *Old Faithful*. It was lump in the throat time.

Although this was one time when the occasion was more important than the match both teams were eager for a victory. Hull obviously wanted to bring down The Boulevard curtain on a successful note and New Zealand needed to get their long-awaited tour off with a win. Both coaches later confirmed that the unusually emotional circumstances made it a unique experience for all concerned. Hull's Shaun McRae said: 'Our guys were pretty relaxed. We didn't get too nervy or built up about it. But I've got to say every man wanted to play in this game and the players who didn't make the team were very disappointed. It was an event they wanted to perform well in and I think they did that.' Kiwi coach Gary Freeman fielded several youngsters and said: 'There were a lot of babies out there playing in front of a massive partisan crowd. That is going to be intimidating for anyone, but I thought they handled the pressure pretty well.'

In fact, Freeman fielded one of his strongest line-ups and only three of the seventeen-man squad did not play in any of the tour's three Test matches against Great Britain. The main absentee was the tour captain and scrum-half Stacey Jones. Hull were also two or three players below full strength. Lee Jackson, Hull's long-serving and popular hooker who had been controversially omitted from their squad for the following season, was given the honour of captaining the Airlie Birds for this historic match. The thirty-three-year-old former Test player was considered by McRae to be ready for retirement, but he turned in a vintage performance that included the setting up of Hull's first try and a couple of characteristic midfield breaks.

Hull 11
  Tries: Horne, Parker
  Goal: Crowther
  Drop goal: Mackay

New Zealand 28
  Tries: Fa'afili (2), Vagana, Vaeliki, Meli
  Goals: Hohaia (4)

Hull players line up after the last match at The Boulevard. Several have swapped into New Zealand kit.

Although played at a fast and furious pace, discipline on both sides was very good with the small penalty count just favouring Hull 7-6. Ironically, for all the great tries scored at The Boulevard over the years the last match's most memorable score was a mighty drop goal by Graham Mackay that must have been one of the longest ever kicked on the ground. Taken just a step or two inside his own half near the centre spot it was reckoned to be 51 metres from kick to posts. It was a spur of the moment decision by the big Australian centre, who let fly with just a few seconds of the first half remaining and the goal gave Hull a 7-6 interval lead. Remarkably, the only other drop goal Mackay had scored was for Penrith in Australia eleven years earlier. The one-point lead was no more than Hull deserved. Despite the early loss of full-back Steve Prescott with a badly sprung shoulder, they had set a terrific pace right from the start and went ahead after only five minutes. Jackson took advantage of the Kiwis' eagerness to move up in defence by pushing through a short kick and Richard Horne dived for the touchdown. Matt Crowther tagged on the goal.

Hull began to get on top with their forwards and backs making rapid progress as the Kiwis took time to settle. The Airlie Birds continued to harry and hound the tourists into a succession of mistakes before the tourists finally made the ball stick and former Boulevarder Michael Smith sent Clinton Toopi leaping over a grounded defender before he put in David Vaeliki near the posts. Lance Hohaia's goal made it

---

Hull: Prescott: Parker, Horne, Mackay, Crowther; J. Smith, T. Smith; Greenhill, L. Jackson, Maher, Logan, Ryan, Chester. Subs: King, Poucher, Fletcher, Cooke (all played).

New Zealand: Vaeliki; Fa'afili, Vagana, Toopi, Meli; Tony, Hohaia; J. Cayless, Betham, Rauhihi, Puletua, Wiki, Swann. Subs: M. Smith, Swain, Guttenbeil, Kearney (all played).

HULL FC v. NEW ZEALAND

A panoramic view of The Boulevard during Hull's last match at the stadium.

6-6 until Mackay's booming drop goal edged Hull ahead at the interval. The introduction of Test hooker Richard Swain early in the second half gave New Zealand's attack more impetus and within ten minutes they went in front. Hohaia seized on a Hull error near halfway to twice kick ahead and Henry Fa'afili won the race to touch down. Eight minutes later Nigel Vagana touched down his own kick that the video referee confirmed as a try. Hohaia added the goal and the Kiwis were flying. A little later long cross-field passing ended with Owen Guttenbeil providing Fa'afili with his second touchdown and Hohaia's goal extended the visitors' lead to 22 points as Hull began to fade. The last opposition try scored at The Boulevard came in the sixty-seventh minute when Francis Meli intercepted Paul Cooke's pass and raced 90 unopposed metres to the posts. Hohaia's simple conversion was the last goal scored against Hull at the ground.*

However, Hull's Paul Parker was to have the distinction of scoring the last Boulevard try. It could not have been stage managed better as, incredibly, he touched down just ten seconds from the end of 107 years of Hull's reign at the old ground. It was a try worthy of the occasion. The countdown was about to begin when Craig Greenhill lobbed over a short kick. Parker caught it on the full 20 metres out and the winger swept round Vaeliki in classic wing style to dive over in the corner. Jackson was given the chance to add the final points with a rare kick at goal, but he was well off target.

And that was it. The Boulevard's round-up days were over. Time for *Old Faithful* to move on to fresh pastures, at the new and ultra-modern Kingston Communications Stadium.

*Although it was Hull's last match at The Boulevard, the ground continued to be used for amateur matches.